PyTorch Cookbook

100+ Solutions put into practice across RNNs, CNNs, PyTorch tools, distributed training and graph networks

AF515805

Matthew Rosch

Published by: GitforGits
www.gitforgits.com
support@gitforgits.com

Printed in India

First Printing: October 2023

ISBN: 978-8119177967

Cover Design by: Kitten Publishing

Prologue

The introduction to "PyTorch Cookbook" prepares readers for an exciting journey into the fascinating realms of deep learning and neural networks, with PyTorch as a foundation. Presenting itself as more than just a book, it leads its readers by the hand and shows them the ropes as they navigate the challenging terrain of machine learning and AI.

The current era is defined by the exponential development of both information and technology. The ever-increasing capabilities of deep learning and artificial intelligence are changing entire markets and expanding the boundaries of possibility. PyTorch is the shining star at the epicentre of this technological renaissance, luring professionals and amateurs alike. However, the abundance of information can be overwhelming, and the road to mastery may seem paved with obstacles, just as it would be in any dynamic field. The goal of the "PyTorch Cookbook" is to make the art and science of deep learning accessible by explaining its complexities and making them easier to understand.

This book is more than just a collection of algorithms and codes; it is also a thoughtful assemblage of useful advice and examples. Its goal is to give readers a firm grasp of the fundamentals of PyTorch and the confidence to apply what they've learned in practical situations. Beginning with tensors and computational graphs, this book introduces the fundamental building blocks of PyTorch and sets the stage for the challenges that lie ahead. From simple feedforward networks to more advanced Convolutional Neural Networks, Recurrent Neural Networks, and Graph Neural Networks, this book covers them all. The inclusion of relevant real-world examples and applications alongside theoretical concepts improves the learning experience and makes the material more memorable.

However, the "PyTorch Cookbook" is not just for one person to study from. It takes into account the rising demand for remote education and scalability, getting readers ready for group efforts and widespread rollouts. To foretell the future of AI in mobile devices, it explores cutting-edge fields like mobile and embedded development. The chapters are structured around troubleshooting and error handling to better prepare readers for potential project roadblocks.

The wider PyTorch ecosystem is one of the book's distinguishing features. Readers will learn about and see examples of using ONNX Runtime, PySyft, Pyro, Deep Graph Library (DGL), Fastai, and Ignite, among other tools and libraries. The book emphasises the need to keep up with technological developments, and these chapters do just that by showcasing the boundless opportunities that lie ahead.

Content

Preface

Starting a PyTorch Developer and Deep Learning Engineer career? Check out this 'PyTorch Cookbook,' a comprehensive guide with essential recipes and solutions for PyTorch and the ecosystem. The book covers PyTorch deep learning development from beginner to expert in well-written chapters.

The book simplifies neural networks, training, optimisation, and deployment strategies chapter by chapter. The first part covers PyTorch basics, data preprocessing, tokenization, and vocabulary. Next, it builds CNN, RNN, Attentional Layers, and Graph Neural Networks. The book emphasises distributed training, scalability, and multi-GPU training for real-world scenarios. Practical embedded systems, mobile development, and model compression solutions illuminate on-device AI applications. However, the book goes beyond code and algorithms. It also offers hands-on troubleshooting and debugging for end-to-end deep learning development. 'PyTorch Cookbook' covers data collection to deployment errors and provides detailed solutions to overcome them.

This book integrates PyTorch with ONNX Runtime, PySyft, Pyro, Deep Graph Library (DGL), Fastai, and Ignite, showing you how to use them for your projects. This book covers real-time inferencing, cluster training, model serving, and cross-platform compatibility. You'll learn to code deep learning architectures, work with neural networks, and manage deep learning development stages. 'PyTorch Cookbook' is a complete manual that will help you become a confident PyTorch developer and a smart Deep Learning engineer. Its clear examples and practical advice make it a must-read for anyone looking to use PyTorch and advance in deep learning.

In this book you will get:

- Comprehensive introduction to PyTorch, equipping readers with foundational skills for deep learning.
- Practical demonstrations of various neural networks, enhancing understanding through hands-on practice.
- Exploration of Graph Neural Networks (GNN), opening doors to cutting-edge research fields.
- In-depth insight into PyTorch tools and libraries, expanding capabilities beyond core functions.
- Step-by-step guidance on distributed training, enabling scalable deep learning and AI projects.
- Real-world application insights, bridging the gap between theoretical knowledge and practical execution.

- Focus on mobile and embedded development with PyTorch, leading to on-device AI.
- Emphasis on error handling and troubleshooting, preparing readers for real-world challenges.
- Advanced topics like real-time inferencing and model compression, providing future-ready skills.

GitforGits

Prerequisites

This book is designed for readers from all walks of life, whether a seasoned professional looking to expand their skillset, an academic seeking to delve deeper into research, or a beginner taking their first steps into the world of AI. Knowing basics of machine learning is preferred.

Codes Usage

Are you in need of some helpful code examples to assist you in your programming and documentation? Look no further! Our book offers a wealth of supplemental material, including code examples and exercises.

Not only is this book here to aid you in getting your job done, but you have our permission to use the example code in your programs and documentation. However, please note that if you are reproducing a significant portion of the code, we do require you to contact us for permission.

But don't worry, using several chunks of code from this book in your program or answering a question by citing our book and quoting example code does not require permission. But if you do choose to give credit, an attribution typically includes the title, author, publisher, and ISBN. For example, "PyTorch Cookbook by Matthew Rosch".

If you are unsure whether your intended use of the code examples falls under fair use or the permissions outlined above, please do not hesitate to reach out to us at support@gitforgits.com.

We are happy to assist and clarify any concerns.

Acknowledgement

I owe a tremendous debt of gratitude to GitforGits, for their unflagging enthusiasm and wise counsel throughout the entire process of writing this book. Their knowledge and careful editing helped make sure the piece was useful for people of all reading levels and comprehension skills. In addition, I'd like to thank everyone involved in the publishing process for their efforts in making this book a reality. Their efforts, from copyediting to advertising, made the project what it is today.

Finally, I'd like to express my gratitude to everyone who has shown me unconditional love and encouragement throughout my life. Their support was crucial to the completion of this book. I appreciate your help with this endeavour and your continued interest in my career.

Acknowledgement

CHAPTER 1: INTRODUCTION TO PYTORCH 2.0

Getting Started

The first part of this excursion has been thoughtfully crafted to provide a solid foundation for everything that lies ahead in the fields of deep learning and artificial intelligence using PyTorch. This introductory chapter serves as an anchor by providing the essential information and tools that one needs in order to get started with PyTorch, regardless of how much prior experience one may or may not have had. In addition to serving as an introduction, this chapter also functions as a map, leading you step-by-step through the various components of PyTorch 2.0. It prepares you to delve deeper into the advanced topics that are presented by covering topics such as installation, tensors, GPUs, gradients, model building, testing, TorchScript, and visualization. This gives you the tools, understanding, and confidence they need to do so. This chapter has been carefully crafted to serve as both a comprehensive starting point and a lasting reference for readers as they continue on their journey with PyTorch. PyTorch's core ideas are condensed and organized within it, and the material is laid out in a way that is user-friendly and interesting; as a result, the book is an absolute necessity for anyone who wants to become an expert in this potent deep learning framework.

The readers will gain an understanding of how to set up PyTorch 2.0 in a variety of environments beginning with the installation procedure. This section clarifies the frequently perplexing path of dependencies and system requirements, making certain that each individual possesses the appropriate version of PyTorch in addition to all of the required components.

Understanding tensors is essential for working with data and developing models in PyTorch because they are the framework upon which the programme is built. This section provides a comprehensive understanding of the fundamental operations, types, and functionalities that will be expanded upon in subsequent chapters by delving deeper into the subject matter. By reading this section, you will learn how to use PyTorch tensors to perform fundamental mathematical operations. When you have a firm grasp of these fundamental ideas, you will have an understanding of how PyTorch handles computations, which will be essential when constructing and training complex neural networks.

The utilization of graphics processing units (GPUs) with PyTorch is the topic of interest in this section. Understanding how to use GPUs through CUDA can significantly speed up both the model training and inference processes. This is because the computations involved in deep learning are highly parallelizable. This section explains how to access the vast computational resources offered by modern GPUs and provides the necessary instructions.

The computation of gradients, which are fundamental to the process of optimizing neural networks, is made easier by the autograd library found in PyTorch. This section provides an explanation of how gradients are automatically calculated, thereby equipping you with the knowledge necessary to construct computation graphs that are both flexible and dynamic. Moving on from the theoretical to the practical, this section will walk you through the process of developing your very first neural network using PyTorch. This hands-on approach helps in understanding the structure and flow of a PyTorch model, covering the definition, training, and evaluation stages of the process respectively.

It is essential to conduct thorough testing and validation when working in the field of machine learning. In this section, you are provided with information regarding the splitting of datasets, the evaluation of model performance, and the utilization of appropriate validation techniques to ensure that models generalize well to data that has not yet been seen. TorchScript provides a method for serializing PyTorch models, which enables these models to run in an environment that does not support Python. You will learn how to make your models more portable and versatile after reading this section, which provides an introduction to a powerful feature.

TensorBoard is a visualization tool that can be integrated with PyTorch, and this chapter concludes with learnings of TensorBoard. It is helpful for both the intuitive understanding of models and the debugging of them to have a working knowledge of how to use TensorBoard to visualize training metrics, model graphs, and other data.

PyTorch 2.0 Features and Capabilities

Introduction to PyTorch 2.0

PyTorch 2.0 stands as one of the most popular and capable deep learning frameworks in AI today. Its optimal balance of flexibility, performance, and ecosystem support makes it appealing to everyone from beginners to seasoned practitioners. Let us dive deeper into what makes PyTorch 2.0 unique and why every aspiring or professional AI developer should learn it.

Tensors and Dynamic Computation Graph

At its foundation, PyTorch relies on tensors, multi-dimensional arrays that can leverage GPUs for immense parallelization and speed. But what truly differentiates PyTorch is its dynamic computation graph. Unlike static graph frameworks, PyTorch constructs the graph on-the-fly as code executes. This enables incredible flexibility, allowing practitioners to tweak neural network architectures dynamically without expensive rebuilds. Debugging is far easier by tracking errors and visualizing metrics at each computation step. The dynamic graph is invaluable for research and rapid iteration.

Autograd System

The autograd system is another cornerstone, automatically calculating gradients during model training. This spares developers from manually implementing gradient functions, a tedious and error-prone process. Autograd simplifies training complex neural networks using gradient-based optimization techniques like SGD or Adam. Any architecture can be trained with minimal code changes. This automation makes PyTorch friendly even for non-experts.

GPU Acceleration

By leveraging CUDA and libraries like cuDNN, PyTorch provides seamless GPU acceleration. Computations are parallelized across GPU cores, providing massive speedups for training performance. As datasets and models grow, GPUs enable training times to scale gracefully. PyTorch democratizes access to GPU power, from workstations to cloud services.

Ecosystem and Libraries

PyTorch shines through its ecosystem - Torchvision for computer vision, TorchText for NLP, TorchAudio, and more. These libraries provide datasets, model architectures, training utilities tailored to each domain. They simplify otherwise complex tasks, while staying up-to-date with research advancements. The ecosystem evolves rapidly, driven by a thriving open-source community.

Model Deployment with TorchScript

For production deployment, TorchScript enables serializing PyTorch models into an intermediate representation. This allows them to run efficiently in non-Python environments like C++. Models can be optimized and packaged into mobile/embedded apps, cloud services, or RPC APIs. TorchScript expands PyTorch's capabilities beyond prototyping into real-world applications.

Features of PyTorch 2.0

Improved Performance

At its core, PyTorch 2.0 provides optimizations that boost performance and efficiency. Operations like slicing and indexing are faster. Memory usage is reduced through sharing storage between tensors and efficient representation of scalars. Overall computation is quicker thanks to improvements in the autograd engine and integration with NVIDIA cuDNN and MKL-DNN libraries. Together these enhancements accelerate experimentation and model training.

Enhanced Distributed Training

For large datasets and models, distributed training is a must, and PyTorch 2.0 refines these capabilities. Integration with NCCL and GLOO libraries enables efficient multi-GPU and multi-node distributed training. Technologies like TCP/GLOO provide networking support for training across nodes. Gradient averaging for parameters is handled seamlessly in the background. These features equip PyTorch for production-scale model development.

Native Quantization and Model Optimization

PyTorch now natively supports quantization, allowing models to be compressed for optimized size and speed without substantial accuracy drops. Researchers can experiment with techniques like pruning, dynamic quantization, and quantization-aware training to optimize models. This facilitates deployment to edge devices with limited resources.

Rich Pre-trained Model Zoo

The release significantly expands PyTorch's model zoo with additional state-of-the-art architectures across domains. Practitioners can leverage these pre-trained models as off-the-shelf solutions or starting points for transfer learning. The model zoo saves time and resources while providing high performance baselines for tackling new problems.

Interoperability with ONNX

For model export and deployment across frameworks, PyTorch 2.0 ensures tight integration with ONNX. Models can be exported to the standardized ONNX format for enhanced compatibility. This allows combining PyTorch's flexibility with libraries like TensorFlow and OpenVINO. The seamless ONNX interoperability further extends PyTorch's versatility.

Why PyTorch 2.0?

Research Flexibility

One of the biggest appeals of PyTorch is its dynamic computation graph, which is particularly attractive to the research community. It enables rapid iteration and experimentation by allowing researchers to use standard Python debugging tools. The ability to modify neural network architectures on the fly makes PyTorch convenient for exploring new ideas and hypotheses. Researchers can quickly test theories and tweak models during training without graph rebuilds. This fluidity encourages a smoother transition from research prototyping to production systems. PyTorch empowers researchers with the flexibility they need to push boundaries.

Industry Adoption

Beyond pure research, many industry leaders are adopting PyTorch for its flexibility, performance, and scalability. Tech giants like Facebook, Tesla, Uber, AMD, Nvidia, and Amazon rely on PyTorch for production-scale deployments. Additionally, companies like Apple, Microsoft, and Google utilize PyTorch for research projects. This industry momentum makes learning PyTorch an invaluable asset for those looking to work in AI-driven companies and roles. Given its rapid uptake across domains like autonomous vehicles, healthcare, and finance, having PyTorch skills will open doors to lucrative career opportunities.

Ease of Learning

One aspect that makes PyTorch more accessible, especially for beginners, is its Pythonic nature. Those already familiar with Python will find PyTorch easy to grasp conceptually due to the similarities in syntax and structure. This reduces the learning curve substantially compared to frameworks based on non-Python environments like C++ or Java. At the same time, PyTorch does not compromise on advanced features, making it suitable for experts as well. The combination of a gentle learning ramp plus extensive capabilities is enticing for learners at all levels, from students to seasoned practitioners.

Alignment with Latest AI Trends

A key benefit of PyTorch is that it evolves rapidly alongside the latest AI research and industry needs. New features for cutting-edge techniques like transformers, reinforcement learning, and generative adversarial networks get incorporated frequently. This keeps PyTorch aligned with the bleeding edge of innovation. By mastering PyTorch 2.0, practitioners can stay current with new developments and leverage them for their projects. Learning PyTorch opens the door to engaging with the latest methodologies and having the tools to implement them.

Versatility in Applications

PyTorch shines in its versatility across problem domains. It powers innovations in computer vision, natural language processing, speech recognition, and more. Researchers harness PyTorch for advancing state-of-the-art in language models like GPT-3, image classifiers, question answering systems, and other complex tasks. Beyond research, it enables building performant, scalable systems for real-world deployment. This vast scope, from cutting-edge research to mission-critical production, is enabled by PyTorch's flexibility. It is a Swiss Army knife applicable to a wide array of challenges in the AI space and beyond.

Whether one is just starting in deep learning or is a seasoned professional pushing the boundaries of AI, PyTorch 2.0 offers the tools, community, and philosophy to foster growth, innovation, and success. Its features are more than mere technical specifications; they represent a commitment to making deep learning accessible, efficient, and profoundly impactful. In embracing PyTorch 2.0, one is not merely adopting a tool but joining a movement that strives to make AI not just a field of scientific inquiry but a canvas of human creativity and potential.

Installing PyTorch 2.0 on Linux

System Requirements

Before beginning the installation, it's crucial to ensure that your Linux system meets the necessary requirements. The given below is what you need:

- Operating System: Ubuntu 16.04 or higher is recommended.
- Python: Python 3.6 or above is necessary. PyTorch is compatible with Python 3.9 as well.
- CUDA: If you plan to use GPU acceleration, make sure your system has an appropriate NVIDIA GPU, and you have the relevant CUDA version installed.

Installing Dependencies

Before installing PyTorch, several dependencies must be in place:

- Python: If you don't have Python installed, you can install it using the following commands:

```
sudo apt update
sudo apt install python3
sudo apt install python3-pip
```

- CUDA (Optional): If you plan to use GPU acceleration, follow the instructions on the official CUDA installation documentation.

Creating Virtual Environment (Optional)

Creating a virtual environment allows you to isolate the PyTorch installation from other Python packages, avoiding potential conflicts. The given below is how to set up a virtual environment using venv:

```
python3 -m venv myenv
source myenv/bin/activate
```

You'll see the environment name (myenv) in your terminal prompt, indicating that the virtual environment is active.

Installing PyTorch via Pip

With the dependencies in place, you can install PyTorch using Python's package manager, pip. Choose the installation command based on your CUDA version:

- For CPU only:

```
pip install torch torchvision torchaudio
```

- For Specific CUDA Version (e.g., CUDA 11.1):

```
pip install torch torchvision torchaudio -f
https://download.pytorch.org/whl/cu111/torch_stable.html
```

Verifying Installation

After the installation, you can verify that PyTorch is installed correctly by running the following Python code:

```
import torch
print(torch.__version__)
print(torch.cuda.is_available())
```

This should print the PyTorch version and a Boolean indicating whether CUDA is available.

Troubleshooting Common Issues

When learning a new framework like PyTorch, users may encounter certain problems during setup and usage. Given below are some common issues and potential solutions:

Compatibility Issues

If PyTorch is throwing errors during import or model training, first ensure compatibility between the Python and CUDA versions with PyTorch 2.0 requirements. Check the official website for the matrix of supported configurations. Using incorrect versions is a prime cause of import and runtime crashes. Create separate Conda/virtualenv environments for different PyTorch versions to avoid conflicts.

Virtual Environment Activation

A common pitfall is forgetting to activate the Conda or virtualenv environment before importing PyTorch and running code. This can manifest in mysterious unresolved imports or missing packages. Always activate the environment first and verify PyTorch imports correctly. Deactivate and reactivate environments if issues arise after new package installations.

CUDA Installation

PyTorch relies on CUDA libraries to leverage NVIDIA GPUs. Errors like "CUDA unavailable" usually imply the CUDA toolkit was not installed correctly. Double-check installation steps and confirm the CUDA path is added to system PATH and LD_LIBRARY_PATH variables. Test CUDA separately using NVIDIA sample codes before attempting PyTorch operations. Reinstall CUDA if issues persist.

Insufficient Memory

Some GPU-related errors like "out of memory" or crashes may stem from insufficient GPU memory for large batches or models. Try reducing batch size or model parameters. Also, check graphics drivers are up to date. Upgrade to more capable GPUs like NVIDIA's high memory models for larger data volumes.

Corrupted Installation

In rare cases, a broken PyTorch install can cause odd behaviors like missing modules or attributes in torch. This may require a clean reinstall after uninstalling existing packages related to PyTorch and CUDA. Pip may cache old packages, so try pip install with --no-cache-dir. Finally, update Python and pip to their latest versions before reinstalling PyTorch.

Additional Tools and Libraries

Once PyTorch is installed, you might also want to install additional tools that are commonly used with PyTorch:

- TorchVision: For working with images (already installed with PyTorch).
- TorchText: For natural language processing, install using pip install torchtext.
- TensorBoard: For visualization, install using pip install tensorboard.

Installing PyTorch 2.0 on Linux is a straightforward process, but attention to detail is vital. Furthermore, the guidance on troubleshooting common issues ensures that even if problems arise, solutions are at hand. The additional information about related tools and updating PyTorch completes the process, providing everything needed for a successful PyTorch 2.0 installation on Linux.

Create and Verify Tensors

Tensors are the fundamental data structures and building blocks in PyTorch. They function as multi-dimensional arrays that can store and operate on data for computations. Tensors provide a powerful, unified framework for all kinds of numerical data, from scalars and vectors to matrices and higher-order representations. Importantly, tensors can utilize both CPUs and GPUs seamlessly, making them essential for accelerated computing. Nearly all deep learning operations rely on tensors, right from simple arithmetic to training sophisticated neural network models. Tensors encapsulate the underlying data arrays as well as attributes like data types and device placement. They accelerate numerical computations by parallelizing across multiple CPUs or GPU cores. PyTorch tensors unlock fast vector/matrix operations, broadcast semantics, automatic differentiation and more. Whether implementing linear regression or convolutional neural networks, PyTorch tensors enable manipulating rich datasets and drive the underlying computations. Mastering tensor operations is key to harnessing PyTorch's capabilities for building performant models. The tensor abstraction simplifies mathematical expressions, allows array-oriented thinking and provides accelerated computation for fast model development and training.

Understanding Tensors

Before diving into the creation of tensors, it's important to grasp what tensors are and how they are structured:

1. Scalars: Zero-dimensional tensors.
2. Vectors: One-dimensional tensors.
3. Matrices: Two-dimensional tensors.
4. Higher-dimensional Tensors: Three or more dimensions.

Creating Tensors

PyTorch offers various ways to create tensors. Given below are the main ones:

Creating Tensors from Data

You can create tensors from lists or NumPy arrays:

```
# From a list
tensor_from_list = torch.tensor([1, 2, 3])

# From a NumPy array
import numpy as np
array = np.array([1, 2, 3])
tensor_from_array = torch.from_numpy(array)
```

Creating Tensors with Specific Values

PyTorch provides functions to create tensors filled with specific values:

1. Zeros: torch.zeros(size)
2. Ones: torch.ones(size)
3. Random Values: torch.rand(size)

Here, size is a tuple defining the dimensions of the tensor.

```
zeros_tensor = torch.zeros((2, 2))
ones_tensor = torch.ones((2, 3))
random_tensor = torch.rand((3, 3))
```

Creating Tensors with Specific Data Types

You can also specify the data type of the tensor using the dtype argument:

```
float_tensor = torch.tensor([1, 2, 3], dtype=torch.float32)
int_tensor = torch.tensor([1, 2, 3], dtype=torch.int32)
```

Tensor Properties

Understanding the properties of a tensor is key to working with them effectively. Given below is how to access these properties:

- Shape: The dimensions of the tensor. Accessed with tensor.shape.
- Data Type: The type of values contained. Accessed with tensor.dtype.
- Device: The hardware device (CPU or GPU) on which the tensor is stored. Accessed with tensor.device.

Verifying Tensor Creation

To ensure that a tensor has been created successfully, you can verify its properties and visualize its content.

Printing Tensor

Simply printing the tensor shows its values:

```
print(tensor_from_list)
```

Checking Shape, Data Type, and Device

You can verify the tensor's properties to ensure they match your expectations:

```
print(tensor_from_list.shape)  # Prints the shape
print(tensor_from_list.dtype)  # Prints the data type
```

```
print(tensor_from_list.device) # Prints the device
```

Manipulating Tensors

Creating tensors is just the beginning. Given below are some common tensor operations:

- Reshaping: Changing the shape of a tensor using tensor.reshape(new_shape).
- Slicing: Accessing parts of the tensor using standard Python slicing.
- Arithmetic Operations: Addition, subtraction, etc., using standard arithmetic operators.
- Matrix Operations: Matrix multiplication, transposition, etc.

Moving Tensors between CPU and GPU

If you have a GPU, you can move tensors between the CPU and GPU:

```
# Moving to GPU
tensor_gpu = tensor_from_list.to('cuda')

# Moving back to CPU
tensor_cpu = tensor_gpu.to('cpu')
```

Interoperability with NumPy

PyTorch tensors can be easily converted to and from NumPy arrays, facilitating interoperability:

```
# Converting a PyTorch tensor to a NumPy array
numpy_array = tensor_from_list.numpy()

# Converting a NumPy array to a PyTorch tensor
tensor_from_numpy = torch.from_numpy(numpy_array)
```

The ability to create and manipulate tensors unlocks the full potential of PyTorch, enabling powerful computations, complex models, and cutting-edge research and applications. The operations and techniques detailed in this section are foundational, serving as both tools and stepping stones to the fascinating world of deep learning.

Tensor Operations

Tensor-matrix multiplication is a core operation in deep learning and scientific computing. It's used in various contexts, including neural network layers, transformations, and solving linear equations. In PyTorch, performing tensor-matrix multiplication is straightforward and optimized for efficiency. This section will walk you through the process, covering various aspects of tensor-matrix multiplication in PyTorch.

Understanding Tensor-Matrix Multiplication

One of the most fundamental tensor operations is matrix multiplication. However, it can take on different forms depending on the rank and dimensions of the tensors involved. Understanding these variants is key to multiplying tensors correctly:

Matrix-Matrix Multiplication

This involves multiplying two 2D matrices together, with the number of columns in the first matrix matching the number of rows in the second. Both operands are rank 2 tensors. Broadcasting is applied if the matrices differ in dimensions. The output is a 2D tensor representing the result.

Matrix-Vector Multiplication

In this case, a 2D matrix is multiplied with a 1D vector. The number of columns in the matrix must equal the length of the vector. The second operand is a rank 1 tensor. The output is a rank 1 tensor representing the resulting vector.

Batch Matrix-Matrix Multiplication

For training neural networks, multiplication occurs between batches of matrices rather than individual matrices. The first operand is a rank 3 tensor containing a batch of matrices. The second operand is a rank 2 tensor representing a single matrix. Broadcasting is applied. The output is a rank 3 tensor containing the batch of multiplied matrices.

The @ operator overloaded for matrix multiplication handles these cases seamlessly based on operand shapes. Paying attention to tensor ranks and dimensions is crucial for multiplying tensors correctly. The appropriate variant is applied automatically based on the inputs. Handling batches of matrices makes PyTorch well-suited for deep learning workloads.

Performing Matrix-Matrix Multiplication

To multiply two matrices, you can use the torch.mm function or the @ operator:

```
import torch

A = torch.tensor([[1, 2], [3, 4]])
B = torch.tensor([[5, 6], [7, 8]])

# Using torch.mm
result = torch.mm(A, B)

# Using the @ operator
result_alternative = A @ B
```

Performing Matrix-Vector Multiplication

Matrix-vector multiplication can be performed using the same functions or operators as matrix-matrix multiplication:

```
A = torch.tensor([[1, 2], [3, 4]])
v = torch.tensor([5, 6])

result = A @ v
```

Performing Batch Matrix-Matrix Multiplication

For batch matrix-matrix multiplication, you can use the torch.bmm function:

```
# Creating batched tensors
A_batch = torch.rand(10, 3, 4) # 10 matrices of size 3x4
B_batch = torch.rand(10, 4, 5) # 10 matrices of size 4x5

result_batch = torch.bmm(A_batch, B_batch) # Result will have shape (10, 3, 5)
```

In-Place Multiplication

If you want to perform the multiplication and store the result in one of the existing tensors, you can use the in-place multiplication functions:

```
A.mm_(B) # Result stored in A
```

Multiplication with Broadcasting

PyTorch supports broadcasting, allowing you to multiply tensors with different shapes, provided certain conditions are met:

```
A = torch.tensor([[1, 2], [3, 4]]) # Shape (2, 2)
B = torch.tensor([5, 6])          # Shape (2,)

result = A @ B.unsqueeze(1)       # Unsqueeze to shape (2, 1), then multiply
```

Ensure that the tensors involved in the multiplication have compatible data types. If not, you may need to convert them using functions like tensor.to(dtype).

If you encounter an error during multiplication, check the following common issues:

- Shape Mismatch: Ensure that the tensor dimensions align correctly.
- Data Type Mismatch: Ensure that the data types are compatible.
- Device Mismatch: Ensure that both tensors are on the same device (CPU or GPU).

Leveraging GPU for Multiplication

If you have access to a GPU, you can perform the multiplication on the GPU for increased speed:

```
A_gpu = A.to('cuda')
B_gpu = B.to('cuda')

result_gpu = A_gpu @ B_gpu
```

Special Matrix Multiplication Functions

PyTorch provides specialized functions for certain types of matrix multiplication. Beyond vanilla matrix multiplication, PyTorch provides some useful functions for specialized variants:

Element-wise Multiplication

For multiplying matrices element-by-element rather than through normal dot products, the torch.mul(A, B) function can be used. This is equivalent to the element-wise multiplication operator: A * B.

Transpose Multiplication

Often we need to multiply the transpose of a matrix with another matrix. This can be done with torch.matmul(A.T, B) which handles transposing matrix A internally before multiplication. An alternative is transposing before the operation: A.T @ B.

Sparse Matrix Multiplication

For multiplying sparse matrices containing mostly zero values, the dedicated torch.sparse.mm() function exists. It avoids computations on zero values for efficiency. Sparse tensors first need to be constructed using torch.sparse_coo_tensor() or other sparse constructors.

Batched Multiplication

Matrices can be stacked into batches for batched multiplication. torch.bmm(A, B) performs batched matrix multiplication between 3D tensors A and B. This is faster than looping over each matrix pair.

These above functions extend matrix multiplication capabilities for specialized use cases like sparse networks or batched training. Along with torch.matmul(), they provide efficient building blocks for linear algebra operations.

Installing CUDA

To utilize the immense parallel processing power of GPUs for accelerated training and inference, PyTorch integrates seamlessly with NVIDIA's CUDA platform. CUDA (Compute Unified Device Architecture) is NVIDIA's parallel computing framework and programming model that enables dramatic speedups by leveraging thousands of GPU cores. It provides low-level GPU control and optimization capabilities to developers.

For deep learning workloads, CUDA Toolkit allows computationally intensive operations to be offloaded to the GPU. This includes things like tensor operations, neural network layers, activation functions, convolution calculations etc. GPU parallelism results in order-of-magnitude faster training and inference compared to CPU-only computations. Along with the CUDA Toolkit, the NVIDIA cuDNN library further optimizes common deep learning primitives. cuDNN accelerates math intensive calculations in popular CNN layers like convolution, pooling, normalization etc.

Given below is a comprehensive practical directions to installing and configuring CUDA to work with PyTorch on a Linux environment.

System Requirements

Before proceeding, ensure that you have a compatible NVIDIA GPU. Check the NVIDIA website for the list of CUDA-enabled GPU models.

Checking for Existing GPU

First, check if your system recognizes the GPU. Open a terminal and run:

```
lspci | grep -i nvidia
```

If your system has an NVIDIA GPU, you will see its details.

Removing Previous NVIDIA Driver Versions

If you have previous versions of the NVIDIA driver installed, it's a good idea to remove them to avoid conflicts:

```
sudo apt-get purge nvidia-*
```

Installing NVIDIA Driver

To utilize CUDA, you must have the appropriate NVIDIA driver installed.

```
sudo add-apt-repository ppa:graphics-drivers/ppa
sudo apt update
```

Find the recommended driver from the NVIDIA website and install it using:

```
sudo apt install nvidia-<driver-number>
Replace <driver-number> with the appropriate driver version.
```

After installing, reboot your system to activate the driver.

Installing CUDA Toolkit

The CUDA Toolkit includes GPU-accelerated libraries, a compiler, development tools, and more.

- Go to the NVIDIA CUDA Toolkit download page and choose the version compatible with your system.

- You can install it using the .deb file:

```
sudo dpkg -i cuda-repo-<ubuntu_version>_<version>_amd64.deb
sudo apt-key adv --fetch-keys
https://developer.download.nvidia.com/compute/cuda/repos/<ubuntu_version>/x86
_64/7fa2af80.pub
sudo apt update
sudo apt install cuda
```

- Replace <ubuntu_version> and <version> with your specific Ubuntu version and the chosen CUDA version.

Configuring Environment Variables

To make CUDA accessible to applications, update the system's PATH and LD_LIBRARY_PATH.

- Open your .bashrc file

```
nano ~/.bashrc
```

- Add the following lines

```
export PATH=/usr/local/cuda/bin:$PATH
export LD_LIBRARY_PATH=/usr/local/cuda/lib64:$LD_LIBRARY_PATH
```

- Source the .bashrc to apply the changes

```
source ~/.bashrc
```

Verifying Installation

To verify that CUDA is installed correctly:

- Check the Driver Version

```
Nvidia-smi
```

- Check the CUDA Version

```
nvcc --version
```

Installing PyTorch with CUDA Support

Finally, make sure to install the PyTorch version compatible with your CUDA version:

```
pip install torch torchvision torchaudio -f
https://download.pytorch.org/whl/cu<cuda_version>/torch_stable.html
```

Replace <cuda_version> with your specific CUDA version (e.g., '101' for CUDA 10.1).

Testing PyTorch with CUDA

You can test PyTorch's CUDA integration with:

```
import torch

print(torch.cuda.is_available()) # Should print True
```

By following these steps, you enable PyTorch to leverage the power of CUDA, unlocking higher computational performance and efficiency. The synergy of CUDA and PyTorch opens up new dimensions in computing capabilities, turning algorithms and ideas into real-world applications and insights. It represents an exciting frontier in computational science, where hardware and software converge, and innovation thrives.

Writing First Neural Network

Developing a basic neural network with PyTorch is an exciting and necessary step in the process of gaining an understanding of how deep learning models function. As was mentioned earlier, you are able to quicken the training process by making use of the power provided by CUDA. In this particular demonstration, you will learn how to build a neural network by utilizing PyTorch and performing common operations, such as tensor manipulation and matrix multiplication, that you are already familiar with.

Importing Libraries and Preparing Data

First, import the necessary libraries and prepare some sample data:

```
import torch
import torch.nn as nn
import torch.optim as optim

# Example tensors from previous section
A = torch.tensor([[1, 2], [3, 4]], dtype=torch.float32)
B = torch.tensor([[5, 6], [7, 8]], dtype=torch.float32)

# Creating dataset
X = torch.cat((A, B), 0) # Inputs
y = torch.tensor([0, 0, 1, 1]) # Labels
```

Defining Neural Network Architecture

You can define a neural network using the nn.Module class. For a simple feedforward network:

```
class SimpleNN(nn.Module):
    def __init__(self, input_size, hidden_size, output_size):
        super(SimpleNN, self).__init__()

        # Layers
        self.fc1 = nn.Linear(input_size, hidden_size)
        self.fc2 = nn.Linear(hidden_size, output_size)

        # Activation function
        self.relu = nn.ReLU()

    def forward(self, x):
        x = self.relu(self.fc1(x))
        x = self.fc2(x)
        return x
```

This network consists of two fully connected layers (nn.Linear) and a ReLU activation function (nn.ReLU).

Creating Neural Network Instance

With the architecture defined, you can create an instance of the network:

```
input_size = 2
hidden_size = 4
output_size = 2

model = SimpleNN(input_size, hidden_size, output_size)

# If CUDA is available, move the model to GPU
if torch.cuda.is_available():
    model = model.cuda()
```

Choosing Loss Function and Optimizer

You need to select a loss function and an optimizer to train the network:

```
criterion = nn.CrossEntropyLoss()
optimizer = optim.Adam(model.parameters(), lr=0.001)
```

Preprocessing Data

For training, it may be useful to convert the labels into a one-hot encoding and move the data to the GPU if available:

```
# Convert to one-hot encoding
y_one_hot = torch.nn.functional.one_hot(y)

# Move data to GPU if available
if torch.cuda.is_available():
    X = X.cuda()
    y_one_hot = y_one_hot.cuda()
```

Training Neural Network

Training involves multiple iterations (epochs) where you calculate the loss, perform backpropagation, and update the weights:

```
epochs = 500

for epoch in range(epochs):
    # Zero the gradients
    optimizer.zero_grad()

    # Forward pass
    outputs = model(X)

    # Compute loss
    loss = criterion(outputs, y)

    # Backward pass
    loss.backward()

    # Update weights
    optimizer.step()

    # Print loss every 50 epochs
    if (epoch + 1) % 50 == 0:
        print(f'Epoch {epoch+1}/{epochs}, Loss: {loss.item()}')
```

Evaluating Model

You can evaluate the model on new data or inspect the outputs for the given inputs:

```
with torch.no_grad():
    outputs = model(X)
    _, predicted = torch.max(outputs, 1)
    print('Predicted:', predicted)
```

Defining the architecture, putting together the training components, and analyzing the model are all steps that are involved in this process. It is a journey that bridges the gap between concepts and applications by transforming mathematical equations and theoretical knowledge into practical understanding. These foundational skills will serve as a solid base as you continue to explore more complex architectures and challenges. They will also enable you to engage with the rich and rapidly evolving field of artificial intelligence.

Testing Neural Networks

The process of developing a model includes several essential steps, including testing and validating a neural network. It is essential to have a solid understanding of how well the model performs on data that it has not previously seen, as this can provide insights into whether the model is overfitting, underfitting, or performing well overall. The following is an in-depth walkthrough that will assist you in testing and validating the neural network model that was developed earlier.

Splitting Data into Training and Testing Sets

First, you need to split the data into training and testing sets to validate the model's performance on unseen data. You can use the train_test_split function from the sklearn.model_selection package to achieve this.

```
from sklearn.model_selection import train_test_split

# Splitting the data
X_train, X_test, y_train, y_test = train_test_split(X.cpu().numpy(), y.cpu().numpy(),
test_size=0.2)

# Converting back to PyTorch tensors
X_train = torch.tensor(X_train, dtype=torch.float32)
X_test = torch.tensor(X_test, dtype=torch.float32)
y_train = torch.tensor(y_train)
y_test = torch.tensor(y_test)

# If CUDA is available, move the data to GPU
if torch.cuda.is_available():
    X_train = X_train.cuda()
    X_test = X_test.cuda()
    y_train = y_train.cuda()
```

```
    y_test = y_test.cuda()
```

Training Model with Training Data

You'll have to retrain the model using only the training data. Refer back to the training loop in the previous section and modify the inputs to use X_train and y_train:

```
# Training loop with X_train and y_train
```

Validating Model on Testing Set

Once the model is trained, you can validate it using the testing set:

```
# Setting the model to evaluation mode
model.eval()

# Forward pass on the test data
with torch.no_grad():
    outputs_test = model(X_test)

# Getting the predicted classes
_, predicted_test = torch.max(outputs_test, 1)

# Converting predictions to a NumPy array
predicted_test = predicted_test.cpu().numpy()

# Printing the predictions
print('Predicted classes on test data:', predicted_test)
```

Calculating Accuracy and Other Metrics

You can evaluate the model's performance by calculating various metrics such as accuracy, precision, recall, and F1-score. The sklearn.metrics module offers functions for these calculations:

```
from sklearn.metrics import accuracy_score, precision_score, recall_score, f1_score
```

```
# Calculating metrics
accuracy = accuracy_score(y_test.cpu().numpy(), predicted_test)
precision = precision_score(y_test.cpu().numpy(), predicted_test, average='macro')
recall = recall_score(y_test.cpu().numpy(), predicted_test, average='macro')
f1 = f1_score(y_test.cpu().numpy(), predicted_test, average='macro')

# Printing the metrics
print('Accuracy:', accuracy)
print('Precision:', precision)
print('Recall:', recall)
print('F1 Score:', f1)
```

Analyzing Results and Making Adjustments

Once the model is trained and tested, it is crucial to thoroughly analyze the results to gauge performance and determine any improvements needed. Examining metrics like accuracy, precision, recall, and F1 score gives a quantitative view of how well the model is predicting the target classes:

- Accuracy indicates the overall percentage of correct predictions made. A high accuracy denotes good performance.
- Precision measures how many of the positive class predictions were actually correct. High precision means few false positives.
- Recall calculates the ratio of positive cases correctly detected. High recall equates to low false negatives.
- F1 score balances both precision and recall into a single metric. It provides a more holistic evaluation.

If the metrics are unsatisfactory, the model likely needs refinement. Given below are some ways to boost model performance:

- Revisit data preprocessing: Applying scaling, normalization, imputation of missing values, or dimensionality reduction on the input data may help.
- Alter model architecture: Try tweaking the number of layers, nodes per layer, activation functions, kernel sizes etc. to improve model capacity.

- Modify training process: Experiment with different optimizers like Adam or SGD, adjust learning rate annealing, batch size, epochs, or other hyperparameters.

- Implement regularization techniques: Methods like dropout, weight decay, or data augmentation can reduce overfitting.

Testing and validation are essential components of model development, helping to ensure that the model generalizes well to new, unseen data. This iterative process of building, testing, and refining is at the heart of machine learning and artificial intelligence, reflecting a pursuit of excellence and a commitment to robust, reliable outcomes.

Getting Started with TorchScript

TorchScript is a way to serialize PyTorch models, making them suitable for deployment in production environments. It provides a robust, flexible way to optimize PyTorch models, allowing them to be run in a non-Python environment. TorchScript also enables some performance improvements by using the Just-In-Time (JIT) compiler to translate the Python code into an intermediate representation that can be optimized and executed efficiently.

Following is a detailed walkthrough to understand TorchScript and how to apply it to the neural network model you have previously developed.

Understanding TorchScript

TorchScript comes in two forms:

- Scripting: By using the torch.jit.script decorator, you can directly compile functions and methods into TorchScript.

- Tracing: The torch.jit.trace function takes a model and an example input, then records the operations that occur when the model is run with that input, creating a TorchScript representation of the model.

Tracing the Model

For most neural networks, tracing is the most straightforward way to convert the model into TorchScript. Let us start by tracing the previously developed model:

```
# Model instance from previous sections
# model = SimpleNN(input_size, hidden_size, output_size)
```

```
# Example input
example_input = torch.rand(1, input_size).cuda() if torch.cuda.is_available() else
torch.rand(1, input_size)

# Tracing the model
traced_model = torch.jit.trace(model, example_input)

# You can now run the traced_model just like a normal PyTorch model
output = traced_model(example_input)
```

Scripting Specific Methods

If you have parts of your model that require more dynamic behavior (e.g., control flow that depends on the input), you may need to use scripting. You can script specific methods within a traced model. Given below is how you might script a method within your SimpleNN class:

```
class SimpleNN(nn.Module):
    # ... (other methods) ...

    @torch.jit.script_method
    def some_dynamic_method(self, x):
        if x.sum() > 0:
            return self.fc1(x)
        else:
            return self.fc2(x)
```

Serializing and Loading Model

You can save the TorchScript model to a file, making it possible to load it later or even in a different environment without Python:

```
# Saving the model
torch.jit.save(traced_model, 'simple_nn_model.pt')

# Loading the model
```

```
loaded_model = torch.jit.load('simple_nn_model.pt')
```

Integrating TorchScript with LibTorch (C++ API)

If you want to run the model in a C++ environment, TorchScript's serialization enables integration with LibTorch, PyTorch's C++ API. You can load and run the TorchScript model in a C++ application:

```
// Loading the model in C++
torch::jit::script::Module module = torch::jit::load("simple_nn_model.pt");

// Running the model in C++
std::vector<torch::jit::IValue> inputs;
inputs.push_back(torch::randn({1, input_size}));
at::Tensor output = module.forward(inputs).toTensor();
```

In this section, you've explored TorchScript and applied it to your existing PyTorch neural network model. Through tracing, scripting, serializing, and potentially integrating with C++ via LibTorch, TorchScript serves as a powerful bridge, connecting the flexibility and ease of PyTorch's Python interface with the robustness, efficiency, and cross-platform capabilities required for production deployment.

Summary

PyTorch 2.0 is currently the industry standard for deep learning frameworks, and this chapter provided you with an introduction to its fundamentals. PyTorch and the CUDA toolkit were both covered, beginning with the installation process, in order to provide GPU support. After that, attention shifted to the process of creating tensors and carrying out fundamental operations such as multiplying tensor matrices, which are fundamental building blocks for more complex deep learning models. The idea of constructing a basic neural network was investigated in great detail, including the critically important facets of training, testing, and validation. These ideas are essential for anyone getting started with deep learning, and the examples that were given helped shed light on the various crucial aspects of the topic.

TorchScript, an essential component for deploying PyTorch models in production environments, was the primary topic of this chapter throughout the chapter's final section. TorchScript makes it easier to serialize models, which enables those models to be optimized and executed in environments where Python is not used. In order to convert the model into TorchScript, tracing and scripting were both explained, and this was followed by an explanation of serialization techniques for saving and loading the model. Real-world applications are now possible thanks to the integration of TorchScript with LibTorch, which is PyTorch's C++ application programming interface. This section revealed how research models can easily transition into robust and efficient production deployments.

In general, the chapter offered a detailed introduction to PyTorch, beginning with installation and progressing all the way up to advanced techniques for production deployment. PyTorch 2.0 provided the reader with the hands-on examples and in-depth illustrations they needed to acquire the skills and knowledge necessary to embark on their deep learning journey using PyTorch 2.0. The practical and theoretical aspects were well-balanced in order to provide a solid understanding, and the step-by-step guidance ensures that even those who are new to in-depth learning will have no trouble understanding these difficult topics. The information that you've gained from this chapter will provide you with a solid basis for advancing your knowledge of PyTorch and applying it to the solution of real-world problems.

CHAPTER 2: DEEP LEARNING BUILDING BLOCKS

Introduction to Deep Learning

Chapter 2 shifts the focus to the building blocks of deep learning, laying the groundwork for understanding the core components that underpin the various models and algorithms. Deep learning mimics the human brain's neural network, and artificial neurons form the basic unit. These neurons take multiple inputs, perform a weighted sum, and pass the result through an activation function. Common activation functions like ReLU, Sigmoid, and Tanh introduce non-linear properties, enabling the neural network to learn complex patterns.

Deep learning models consist of layers of interconnected neurons. There are different types of layers, including:

- Input Layer: Accepts the feature inputs.
- Hidden Layers: Processes the inputs through multiple neurons and layers.
- Output Layer: Generates the final prediction or classification.

The way these layers are structured defines the architecture of a neural network, such as Feedforward, Convolutional Neural Networks (CNN), or Recurrent Neural Networks (RNN).

Loss functions measure the difference between the predicted output and the actual target. It is crucial for training a model as it provides a metric to optimize. Common loss functions include Mean Squared Error for regression and Cross-Entropy for classification.

Optimization algorithms adjust the weights in the network to minimize the loss function. Gradient Descent is a fundamental optimization technique, and its variations like Stochastic Gradient Descent (SGD), Adam, and RMSProp are widely used. They differ in how they update the weights, introducing concepts like momentum and adaptive learning rates.

Regularization helps prevent overfitting, where a model performs well on training data but poorly on unseen data. Techniques such as Dropout, L1/L2 regularization, and early stopping add constraints to the learning process, ensuring that the model generalizes well.

Preparing data appropriately is vital for training successful models. Preprocessing includes normalizing or scaling the features, handling missing values, and encoding categorical variables. Data augmentation creates variations of the training data, enhancing the model's ability to generalize.

Training deep learning models often involves dividing the dataset into batches and iteratively updating the weights over multiple passes (epochs). This approach helps in managing large datasets and introduces concepts like batch normalization.

Understanding these building blocks is essential for anyone working with deep learning. Whether designing a new model or troubleshooting an existing one, recognizing how these components interact helps in making informed decisions and optimizations. This chapter sets the stage for exploring more advanced topics, and the practical examples that follow will apply these principles to real-world problems. The insights gained here also serve as a basis for troubleshooting and fine-tuning models, which will be the focus of subsequent chapters.

Introduction to Linear Layers

Linear layers, also known as fully connected or dense layers, are a fundamental building block of neural network models. They perform a linear transformation on their inputs, making them suitable for learning patterns in data. In this section, you will explore how to apply linear layers to the previous example, extending the simple neural network with additional linear transformations.

Understanding Linear Layers

Linear layers transform input data through a combination of matrix multiplication with a weight matrix and addition of a bias vector. The mathematical representation of a linear layer is:

$$y=xW+b$$

where,

- x is the input,
- W is the weight matrix,
- b is the bias vector, and
- y is the output.

Applying Linear Layers

In PyTorch, linear layers are implemented using the nn.Linear class. Let us revisit the previously created neural network and add more linear layers to it.

Creating Extended Model

```
import torch.nn as nn

class ExtendedNN(nn.Module):
```

```
    def __init__(self, input_size, hidden_size1, hidden_size2, output_size):
        super(ExtendedNN, self).__init__()
        self.fc1 = nn.Linear(input_size, hidden_size1)
        self.fc2 = nn.Linear(hidden_size1, hidden_size2)
        self.fc3 = nn.Linear(hidden_size2, output_size)
        self.relu = nn.ReLU()

    def forward(self, x):
        x = self.fc1(x)
        x = self.relu(x)
        x = self.fc2(x)
        x = self.relu(x)
        x = self.fc3(x)
        return x
```

In the above snippet, we've added two hidden linear layers (fc1 and fc2), followed by the output linear layer (fc3). The ReLU activation function introduces non-linearity between the layers.

Instantiating and Exploring Model

```
input_size = 784  # For example, a 28x28 image
hidden_size1 = 256
hidden_size2 = 128
output_size = 10  # For example, 10 classes in classification

model = ExtendedNN(input_size, hidden_size1, hidden_size2, output_size)
print(model)
```

The printed model architecture would show the three linear layers with their corresponding input and output sizes.

Training Extended Model

Training the extended model follows the same process as before. Define a loss function and an optimizer, then iterate through epochs and batches to update the model's weights.

```
import torch.optim as optim

# Loss and optimizer
criterion = nn.CrossEntropyLoss()
optimizer = optim.Adam(model.parameters(), lr=0.001)

# Training loop (with existing training_data_loader)
for epoch in range(num_epochs):
    for i, (inputs, labels) in enumerate(training_data_loader):
        outputs = model(inputs)
        loss = criterion(outputs, labels)
        optimizer.zero_grad()
        loss.backward()
        optimizer.step()
```

Once trained, the extended model can be used for predictions and validation just like before. The additional linear layers provide more capacity to learn complex patterns from the data.

Adding more linear layers increases the model's ability to capture intricate relationships in the data but also makes the model more prone to overfitting. Proper selection of hidden layer sizes, activation functions, and regularization techniques becomes vital.

Implementing Activation Function

Activation functions play a vital role in neural networks by introducing non-linear properties, allowing the network to learn complex patterns. Without these non-linearities, the entire neural network would behave as a single linear transformation, greatly limiting its expressiveness.

In the previous section, we introduced a neural network with two hidden linear layers. We used the ReLU (Rectified Linear Unit) activation function, but now let us dive deeper into the application of various activation functions, learning why and how they are used.

Understanding Activation Functions

Activation functions are a crucial component of neural networks. They are applied to the summed weighted output of each node in a layer, introducing non-linearity. Without activation functions, neural networks would simply be linear regression models. Following are some key activation functions:

- ReLU (Rectified Linear Unit): This applies the function f(x) = max(0, x). It sets all negative input values to zero while retaining positive values. ReLU adds non-linearity while being simple and fast to compute.

- Sigmoid: The sigmoid function has a characteristic S-shaped curve, squashing real-valued inputs into a range between 0 and 1. It is defined as f(x) = 1 / (1 + exp(-x)). The sigmoid was popular historically but has fallen out of favor due to issues like vanishing gradients.

- Tanh: Tanh (Hyperbolic Tangent) is similar to sigmoid but produces outputs between -1 and 1. It is zero-centered unlike sigmoid. But tanh also suffers from problems like vanishing gradients.

- Softmax: This squashes a vector of arbitrary reals into a vector of probabilities summing up to 1. Softmax is often used in the final layer for multi-class classification problems. It interprets the raw outputs as probabilities for each class.

Implementing Activation Functions in PyTorch

In PyTorch, activation functions are available as separate modules within the torch.nn namespace or as functions within torch.nn.functional.

Let us modify our previous ExtendedNN class by introducing different activation functions.

```
import torch.nn.functional as F

class ExtendedNNWithActivation(nn.Module):
  def __init__(self, input_size, hidden_size1, hidden_size2, output_size):
    super(ExtendedNNWithActivation, self).__init__()
    self.fc1 = nn.Linear(input_size, hidden_size1)
    self.fc2 = nn.Linear(hidden_size1, hidden_size2)
    self.fc3 = nn.Linear(hidden_size2, output_size)

  def forward(self, x):
    x = F.relu(self.fc1(x))  # ReLU after first layer
    x = F.tanh(self.fc2(x))  # Tanh after second layer
    x = self.fc3(x)
    return F.softmax(x, dim=1)  # Softmax for the output layer
```

In this model, we've used ReLU, Tanh, and Softmax activation functions for different layers. Training the model with activation functions follows the same process as before. The inclusion of activation functions allows the network to capture complex relationships in the data, which linear transformations alone cannot achieve. The application of these activation functions can be experimented with the existing data and examples to observe how they impact the learning process, model's performance, and convergence rate.

Minimizing Loss Function

Minimizing the loss function is an essential step in training neural networks, as it ensures the model is learning from the data and making accurate predictions. The process of minimizing the loss is achieved through optimization techniques that adjust the model's weights in a direction that reduces the error.

In this context, you will explore the concept of the loss function, how it is used in training, and the techniques applied to minimize it using the previously created neural model with linear layers and activation functions.

Understanding Loss Function

The loss function quantifies how well the model's predictions match the actual target values. It's a mathematical function that takes the model's predictions and the true labels as inputs and returns a single scalar value representing the error. The goal is to find the model parameters that minimize this error.

Common loss functions in PyTorch include:

- Mean Squared Error (MSE): Used for regression tasks.
- Cross-Entropy Loss: Used for classification tasks.
- Huber Loss: A combination of MSE and MAE (Mean Absolute Error), which is less sensitive to outliers.

Implementing Loss Function in PyTorch

In our previous example, we created a neural network model for classification. For such a task, the Cross-Entropy Loss is typically used. In PyTorch, this can be implemented using the nn.CrossEntropyLoss class.

```
criterion = nn.CrossEntropyLoss()
```

Calculating Loss During Training

During the training loop, the loss is calculated by comparing the model's output to the true labels. Given below is how it fits into our existing training loop:

```
for epoch in range(num_epochs):
    for i, (inputs, labels) in enumerate(training_data_loader):
        outputs = model(inputs)
        loss = criterion(outputs, labels)
        # continue with optimization
```

Optimizing Loss Function

To minimize the loss, we use optimization techniques that adjust the model's weights. The most common methods include:

- Gradient Descent: Adjusts the weights in the direction that reduces the loss.
- Stochastic Gradient Descent (SGD): A variant that computes the gradient using a single or small batch of examples.
- Adam: A popular optimization technique that combines the benefits of other methods.
- In PyTorch, these can be implemented using the torch.optim package:

```
optimizer = torch.optim.Adam(model.parameters(), lr=0.001)
```

Training Loop with Optimization

The complete training loop with loss calculation and optimization is as follows:

```
for epoch in range(num_epochs):
    for i, (inputs, labels) in enumerate(training_data_loader):
        outputs = model(inputs)
        loss = criterion(outputs, labels)
        optimizer.zero_grad()
        loss.backward()  # Compute gradients
        optimizer.step() # Update weights
```

By building upon the previously created neural model, and through hands-on experimentation, you can gain practical insights into the dynamics of loss minimization. The techniques and insights presented here set the stage for more advanced optimization strategies and model evaluation approaches. They provide a robust foundation for ongoing learning and exploration, enabling you to develop increasingly effective and efficient models for complex real-world tasks.

Optimization Techniques

Optimization techniques play a pivotal role in training neural networks, adjusting the model's parameters to minimize the loss function. Various optimization algorithms have been developed, each with its characteristics and suited for different types of problems. In this section, you will explore different optimization techniques and apply one of them to the previously created neural model.

Overview of Optimization Techniques

Training neural networks revolves around minimizing a loss function by tweaking the weights and biases of the model. Optimization algorithms make this process fast and efficient through some key ideas:

Gradient Descent

This fundamental algorithm works by estimating the gradient of the loss function and updating parameters in the negative gradient direction to descend towards a minimum. The learning rate hyperparameter determines the step size. However, vanilla gradient descent can get trapped oscillating around local minima and ravines.

Stochastic Gradient Descent (SGD)

Rather than computing the true gradient over the full dataset, SGD estimates the gradient using only a small randomly selected subset of data points (a minibatch). This introduces noise that helps escape shallow local minima to find deeper ones. However, the randomness also means the path to convergence is less smooth.

Mini-batch SGD

A variation of SGD that takes the best of both worlds - it uses a small minibatch of data to estimate the gradient rather than individual points, smoothing out noise. The minibatch size provides a handy leverage to trade off noise vs efficiency.

Momentum

Momentum accelerates training by accumulating an exponentially decaying moving average of past gradient steps to push optimization consistently in profitable directions. This helps dampen oscillations and break through small barriers and plateaus. Momentum simulates physical inertia - objects in motion tend to stay moving.

Nesterov Accelerated Gradient (NAG)

NAG is a modification to momentum where the gradient is evaluated not w.r.t to the current parameters, but w.r.t the anticipated position after taking the momentum step. This "look-ahead" gradient prevents overshooting near minima.

Adagrad

Adagrad adapts the learning rate dynamically for each parameter based on the history of gradients for that parameter. Infrequently updated parameters get larger updates while frequent ones get smaller updates. But the monotonic learning rate usually decays too quickly.

Adadelta

Adadelta restricts the window of accumulated past gradients to a fixed size, eliminating the radially diminishing learning rates of Adagrad. The update is based on the ratio of the root mean square of the current gradient to the past gradient.

RMSprop

RMSprop takes the idea of adapting learning rates from Adagrad but changes the implementation - it normalizes the gradient by dividing it by a running average of recent magnitudes. This normalized gradient decouples the convergence speed from the absolute learning rate.

Adam

Adam combines ideas from RMSprop and momentum - it calculates running averages of both the gradients and the second moments of the gradients to adaptively control both the step size and acceleration of parameter updates. The result is a smooth yet rapid training process.

Applying Adam Optimizer to Model

Adam is a popular optimization technique and has shown excellent performance across various tasks. You will apply Adam to our previous neural model.

Creating Adam Optimizer

In PyTorch, creating an Adam optimizer is straightforward:

```
optimizer = torch.optim.Adam(model.parameters(), lr=0.001)
```

In the above snippet, model.parameters() gives the parameters that need to be optimized, and lr sets the learning rate.

Training Loop with Adam Optimizer

The training loop remains mostly the same, with the optimizer handling the weight updates:

```
for epoch in range(num_epochs):
    for i, (inputs, labels) in enumerate(training_data_loader):
        outputs = model(inputs)
        loss = criterion(outputs, labels)
        optimizer.zero_grad()  # Reset gradients
        loss.backward()        # Compute gradients
        optimizer.step()       # Update weights
```

Fine-Tuning Adam

Adam's hyperparameters can be fine-tuned:

- Learning Rate: The step size in the direction of the minimum. Typically set between 0.1 and 0.0001

- Beta1 and Beta2: Control the decay rates of the moving averages of the gradient and the squared gradient. Defaults are usually effective (beta1=0.9, beta2=0.999).

Regularization Techniques

Regularization techniques are essential in training robust neural network models. They add specific constraints or penalties to the learning process to prevent overfitting. Overfitting occurs when the model performs well on the training data but poorly on unseen data, making the use of regularization vital in practice.

Overview of Regularization Techniques

L1 Regularization (Lasso)

L1 regularization adds the absolute value of the weights to the loss function. It encourages sparsity, meaning some weights can become exactly zero, effectively removing certain features or connections.

L2 Regularization (Ridge)

L2 regularization adds the square of the weights to the loss function. Unlike L1, it doesn't result in zero weights but instead penalizes large weight values, constraining the model's complexity.

Dropout

Dropout is a regularization method unique to neural networks. During training, randomly selected neurons are ignored, forcing the network to learn redundant representations, thereby enhancing robustness.

Early Stopping

Early stopping involves halting the training process when the model's performance on a validation dataset stops improving. It ensures that the model doesn't overfit the training data.

Weight Decay

Weight decay is related to L2 regularization and penalizes large weights. It can be applied alongside other optimization techniques.

Batch Normalization

Although not strictly a regularization method, batch normalization can have a regularizing effect. It normalizes the activations within a layer, helping with training stability and sometimes reducing the need for other forms of regularization.

Applying Dropout to Model

Dropout is a widely-used regularization technique, particularly effective in large neural networks. You will explore how to apply dropout to the neural model we created earlier.

Implementing Dropout

In PyTorch, Dropout is implemented as a layer. Following is how to add it to a neural network:

```
class NeuralModel(nn.Module):
    def __init__(self):
        super(NeuralModel, self).__init__()
        self.layer1 = nn.Linear(in_features, hidden_features)
        self.dropout = nn.Dropout(p=0.5) # 50% dropout rate
        self.layer2 = nn.Linear(hidden_features, out_features)
```

```
    def forward(self, x):
        x = F.relu(self.layer1(x))
        x = self.dropout(x) # Applying dropout
        x = self.layer2(x)
        return x
```

The parameter p defines the probability of dropping out a neuron. Common values are between 0.2 and 0.5.

Training with Dropout

The training process with dropout remains the same. During training, dropout is active, but during evaluation, it is turned off:

```
model.train() # Enable dropout during training
# Training loop...
model.eval()  # Disable dropout during evaluation
```

Fine-Tuning Dropout

Tuning the dropout rate can be done through cross-validation. It's often beneficial to experiment with different dropout rates to find the one that yields the best validation performance.

Understanding Impact of Dropout

Dropout adds noise to the training process, making the learning more robust:

- Preventing Overfitting: By randomly turning off neurons, the network becomes less reliant on specific weights, reducing overfitting.
- Encouraging Redundancy: The network must learn more robust features, as it can't rely on any single neuron.

Dropout can be used alongside other regularization techniques like L1/L2 regularization or weight decay. By integrating the dropout technique into the previously created model, you've engaged in hands-on learning that reflects real-world deep learning practices.

Creating Custom Layers

Creating and adding custom layers to a neural network is a powerful feature that allows for tailored and specialized architectures. Custom layers are often required to implement novel ideas, unique functions, or specific behaviors within a network. A custom layer is a combination of mathematical operations that transform the input data in a specific way. It can encapsulate complex logic, multiple sub-layers, or unique activation functions. Custom layers provide flexibility and control over the network's architecture.

You will explore how to create and integrate custom layers into the previously created model with PyTorch.

Let us start by defining a custom layer. You will create a layer that performs a linear transformation followed by a specific non-linear activation.

Subclassing nn.Module

In PyTorch, custom layers are created by subclassing nn.Module. Following is the skeleton of a custom layer:

```
import torch.nn as nn

class CustomLayer(nn.Module):
    def __init__(self, ...):
        super(CustomLayer, self).__init__()
        # Initialization code here

    def forward(self, x):
        # Transformation code here
        return x
```

The __init__ method initializes the layer's parameters, and the forward method defines how the input data x is transformed.

Defining Custom Layer's Operations

For our example, you will create a layer that combines a linear transformation with a specific activation function, such as a scaled exponential linear unit (SELU):

```
class CustomLayer(nn.Module):
    def __init__(self, in_features, out_features):
        super(CustomLayer, self).__init__()
```

```
        self.linear = nn.Linear(in_features, out_features)
        self.selu = nn.SELU()

    def forward(self, x):
        x = self.linear(x)
        x = self.selu(x)
        return x
```

In the above snippet, the CustomLayer consists of a linear transformation followed by a SELU activation.

Integrating Custom Layer into Previous Model

Now that we've defined the custom layer, we can integrate it into the previously created model:

```
class NeuralModelWithCustomLayer(nn.Module):
    def __init__(self, in_features, hidden_features, out_features):
        super(NeuralModelWithCustomLayer, self).__init__()
        self.layer1 = CustomLayer(in_features, hidden_features)
        self.dropout = nn.Dropout(p=0.5)
        self.layer2 = nn.Linear(hidden_features, out_features)

    def forward(self, x):
        x = self.layer1(x)
        x = self.dropout(x)
        x = self.layer2(x)
        return x
```

In the above snippet, layer1 is now an instance of our custom layer, adding the specific transformation we designed.

Training and Utilizing Model with Custom Layer

The training process remains the same as before. The custom layer behaves like any other layer in PyTorch, allowing seamless integration.

Custom layers can be as simple or complex as needed. They can include multiple sub-layers, special activation functions, conditional logic, or even trainable parameters. Understanding how to create custom layers opens the door to more advanced and specialized neural network architectures.

Common Challenges & Solutions

In this practical exploration of deep learning, specifically focusing on building neural models with PyTorch, a wide array of errors might arise. These errors can range from issues with data preprocessing to model architecture, training, and even deployment. In this section, we will learn some common errors and provide solutions for them, linked with the activities and concepts covered in this chapter.

Data Preprocessing Errors

Mismatched Dimensions

The input data doesn't match the expected shape of the custom layer or any other layer in the neural network.

Solution - Always verify the dimensions of your input data and ensure that they align with your network's architecture. Using debugging tools and printing shapes at different stages can help in identifying inconsistencies.

Inconsistent Data Types

Mixing different data types, such as floats and integers, within input data or model parameters.

Solution - Do verify that all the tensors have the same data type. Utilize the .to() method in PyTorch to convert tensors to the same type if needed.

Model Architecture Errors

Incompatible Layer Sizes

Problem: Successive layers have incompatible sizes, causing runtime errors during forward propagation.

Solution - Carefully design the layers, making sure that the output size of one layer matches the input size of the next. This applies to custom layers as well.

Wrong Activation Function

Using an inappropriate activation function, causing training to be ineffective.

Solution - Choose activation functions that suit the problem at hand. Understanding the underlying mathematics of activation functions can aid in making informed decisions.

Training Errors

Vanishing or Exploding Gradients

During backpropagation, gradients may become too small (vanishing) or too large (exploding), affecting the training process.

Solution - Utilize proper weight initialization methods, batch normalization, or gradient clipping to control the magnitude of gradients.

Overfitting or Underfitting

The model either performs too well on the training data (overfitting) or too poorly (underfitting), leading to suboptimal generalization.

Solution - Use techniques like regularization (e.g., dropout), early stopping, or proper data splitting to create a balanced model.

Optimization Errors

Improper Learning Rate

Setting the learning rate too high or too low can cause the training to diverge or converge too slowly.

Solution - Experiment with different learning rates or use adaptive learning rate techniques like Adam.

Local Minima

The optimization algorithm might get stuck in a local minimum, leading to suboptimal solutions.

Solution - Utilize momentum-based optimization techniques to overcome local minima.

CUDA and GPU Errors

Memory Overflow

Running out of GPU memory during training or evaluation.

Solution - Reduce the batch size, model complexity, or use gradient accumulation techniques to manage GPU memory efficiently.

Mismatched Device Allocation

Tensors and models are not on the same device (CPU/GPU).

Solution - Ensure that both the model and data are on the same device using .to(device) method.

Custom Layer Errors

Incorrect Forward Pass Implementation

The custom layer's forward paSs is incorrectly implemented, leading to unexpected behavior.

Solution - Test the custom layer independently with known inputs and expected outputs to ensure its correctness.

Failure to Register Parameters

Custom layer parameters are not being trained.

Solution - Ensure that all learnable parameters in a custom layer are registered with nn.Parameter or contained within standard PyTorch modules.

Summary

In this chapter, we began a journey into a comprehensive investigation of the building blocks of deep learning as well as the more advanced modeling techniques using PyTorch. We started by adding linear layers to a neural model, and throughout this process, we were conscious of the importance of maintaining consistent data types and matching dimensions. Integration of Activation Functions Followed by an Emphasis on the Importance of Selecting Appropriate Functions to Enable Effective Training After that, activation functions were integrated. The objective of minimizing the loss function was addressed using a variety of optimization techniques, which enhanced both the learning process and the performance of the model.

We continued our research on regularization techniques and implemented some of those techniques into our model in order to prevent overfitting and underfitting. We discovered the adaptability of PyTorch when it comes to meeting one-of-a-kind and one-of-a-kind requirements through the utilization of custom layers. In order to guarantee compatibility and functionality, the implementation of a custom layer required painstaking design. We were able to delve into the multifaceted challenges that may arise in real-world scenarios by first taking a comprehensive look at possible errors and their solutions. These challenges range from data preprocessing and model architecture all the way to optimisation and GPU handling.

The chapter came to a close with a helpful troubleshooting solutions that concentrated on providing solutions that were immediately applicable to typical problems. This hands-on approach to recognising and resolving issues emphasizes the practical nature of deep learning, thereby providing you with the skills necessary to navigate complex problems and foster robust solutions. Overall, the chapter served as a thorough technical material to constructing and perfecting neural models with PyTorch. It offered a unified and insightful journey through the complex terrain of deep learning.

CHAPTER 3: CONVOLUTIONAL NEURAL NETWORKS

Convolutional Neural Networks Overview

Introduction

Convolutional Neural Networks (CNNs) represent a distinct category of neural networks that have had a profound impact on the realm of computer vision. Originating from the principles of hierarchical pattern theory and inspired by the workings of the visual cortex in biological systems, CNNs are designed to autonomously and dynamically learn a layered structure of features from the input data they receive. In more detail, the architecture of a CNN is structured to emulate how a human eye perceives visual elements, capturing intricate patterns at various scales and complexities. Unlike traditional neural networks, which treat input features as flat vectors, CNNs preserve the spatial relationships between pixels by learning image features using small squares of input data.

The strength of CNNs lies in their ability to identify hierarchical patterns in the data. This begins with the detection of simple features like edges and textures. As the data progresses through deeper layers of the network, the features become more complex, eventually enabling the model to identify shapes, objects, and even entire scenes in some cases. This hierarchical feature learning is what allows CNNs to perform exceptionally well in tasks such as image classification, object detection, and even in areas beyond visual perception like natural language processing and time-series analysis. This layered, hierarchical approach is particularly effective because it doesn't require manual feature extraction, a labor-intensive and often error-prone process. Instead, CNNs perform feature learning automatically, thereby streamlining the model training process and leading to more robust and accurate models. As a result, CNNs have become the go-to architecture for a wide range of applications in computer vision, setting new performance benchmarks and enabling breakthroughs in various domains.

Structure and Functionality

A typical CNN consists of a sequence of layers, each designed to analyze different aspects of the input image. These layers include convolutional layers, pooling (subsampling or down-sampling) layers, fully connected layers, and normalization layers.

- Convolutional Layers: The convolutional layer applies filters to the input image to detect specific features like edges, corners, textures, etc. By sliding these filters across the image, the network can learn to recognize spatial hierarchies and complex shapes.

- Pooling Layers: These layers reduce the dimensionality of the data, preserving essential information while discarding redundant details. This down-sampling process makes the network more robust to variations and distortions in the input image.

- Fully Connected Layers: These layers interpret the higher-order features extracted by the convolutional and pooling layers and perform classification based on the identified patterns.

Usage and Applications

CNNs are widely used to classify images into predefined categories. From identifying objects in pictures to detecting diseases in medical scans, their application spans various domains. Beyond simple classification, CNNs can locate and outline specific objects within an image, essential for autonomous driving, surveillance, and more.

Generative models like GANs (Generative Adversarial Networks) use CNNs to produce new, synthetic instances of images that can resemble real photos. As technology advances, CNNs will likely play a crucial role in real-time analysis, vital for augmented reality, real-time medical diagnosis, etc. Through continuous learning and adaptation, CNNs could offer highly personalized services, such as tailored content recommendations or personalized healthcare. CNNs may be utilized for large-scale environmental monitoring, analyzing satellite imagery to detect changes in ecosystems, predict natural disasters, and more. With growing concerns about ethics in AI, future research may focus on creating transparent, accountable, and bias-free CNN models.

CNNs have radically changed the way computers perceive and interpret visual information. They have become the cornerstone of modern computer vision, extending their reach beyond mere image recognition into complex tasks like object detection, segmentation, and even image synthesis. As technology evolves, the potential applications and innovations stemming from CNNs are bound to expand, offering a glimpse into a future where machines not only see but understand and interact with the world in a human-like manner.

My First CNN

Building a Convolutional Neural Network (CNN) can be an exciting journey, especially when you have a grasp of its underlying theory. Now, you will practically implement a simple yet powerful CNN using PyTorch, continuing with our previous neural network model as a basis.

Importing Necessary Libraries

First, let us import the necessary libraries and modules. PyTorch and its associated libraries provide all the required functionality.

```
import torch
import torch.nn as nn
import torch.optim as optim
```

```
import torchvision.datasets as datasets
import torchvision.transforms as transforms
from torch.utils.data import DataLoader
```

Loading Data

For this particular program, you will continue with the MNIST dataset used previously. The transforms are applied to preprocess the data.

```
train_data = datasets.MNIST(root='data', train=True, download=True,
transform=transforms.ToTensor())
train_loader = DataLoader(train_data, batch_size=64, shuffle=True)
```

Defining CNN Architecture

You will create a simple CNN with two convolutional layers, followed by pooling layers, and two fully connected layers.

```
class CNN(nn.Module):
  def __init__(self):
    super(CNN, self).__init__()
    self.layer1 = nn.Sequential(
      nn.Conv2d(1, 32, kernel_size=3, stride=1, padding=1),
      nn.ReLU(),
      nn.MaxPool2d(kernel_size=2, stride=2)
    )
    self.layer2 = nn.Sequential(
      nn.Conv2d(32, 64, kernel_size=3),
      nn.ReLU(),
      nn.MaxPool2d(2)
    )
    self.fc1 = nn.Linear(64 * 6 * 6, 1000)
    self.fc2 = nn.Linear(1000, 10)

  def forward(self, x):
```

```
        x = self.layer1(x)
        x = self.layer2(x)
        x = x.view(x.size(0), -1)
        x = self.fc1(x)
        x = self.fc2(x)
        return x
```

In the above snippet, nn.Conv2d is used to create convolutional layers, and nn.MaxPool2d is applied for pooling. Fully connected layers are implemented using nn.Linear.

Instantiating Model, Loss Function, and Optimizer

Now, instantiate the model, loss function, and optimizer.

```
model = CNN()
criterion = nn.CrossEntropyLoss()
optimizer = optim.Adam(model.parameters(), lr=0.001)
```

Training Model

You will train the model using our training data.

```
for epoch in range(10): # Training for 10 epochs
    for images, labels in train_loader:
        outputs = model(images)
        loss = criterion(outputs, labels)
        optimizer.zero_grad()
        loss.backward()
        optimizer.step()
```

You should now have a fundamental CNN built with PyTorch after following the steps outlined in this hands-on sample program. We have organized the network so that it consists of two layers that are convolutional, two layers that are pooling, and two layers that are fully connected. This implementation of a CNN should provide a solid foundation for more complex models and applications in computer vision by building upon the prior example and understanding.

Explore GoogLeNet

The GoogLeNet architecture, alternatively referred to as Inception v1, stands as a landmark development in the domain of Convolutional Neural Networks (CNNs). This architecture gained attention for its innovative structure known as the "Inception Module," which allows for a dramatic expansion in both the depth and width of the neural network without correspondingly inflating the computational burden.

Understanding Inception Module

The core idea behind GoogLeNet's Inception Module is to have a network decide how to perform the best convolution operation rather than manually fine-tuning filter sizes and operations.

An Inception Module consists of:

Convolutional Layers with different kernel sizes (1x1, 3x3, 5x5) to capture various spatial characteristics.

- Pooling Layer: Usually, a max-pooling layer with a 3x3 kernel.
- 1x1 Convolutional Layers for Dimension Reduction: These reduce the computational complexity without losing essential features.

The outputs from these parallel operations are concatenated, forming the output of the Inception Module.

Implementing GoogLeNet with PyTorch

You will create a simple version of GoogLeNet with PyTorch, focusing on the implementation of the Inception Module.

Import Libraries

```
import torch.nn as nn
```

Define Inception Module

```
class InceptionModule(nn.Module):
    def __init__(self, in_channels):
```

```
        super(InceptionModule, self).__init__()

        # 1x1 Convolution
        self.branch1 = nn.Conv2d(in_channels, 16, kernel_size=1)

        # 1x1 Convolution followed by 3x3 Convolution
        self.branch2 = nn.Sequential(
            nn.Conv2d(in_channels, 16, kernel_size=1),
            nn.Conv2d(16, 24, kernel_size=3, padding=1)
        )

        # 1x1 Convolution followed by 5x5 Convolution
        self.branch3 = nn.Sequential(
            nn.Conv2d(in_channels, 16, kernel_size=1),
            nn.Conv2d(16, 24, kernel_size=5, padding=2)
        )

        # 3x3 Max-Pooling followed by 1x1 Convolution
        self.branch4 = nn.Sequential(
            nn.MaxPool2d(kernel_size=3, stride=1, padding=1),
            nn.Conv2d(in_channels, 24, kernel_size=1)
        )

    def forward(self, x):
        branch1 = self.branch1(x)
        branch2 = self.branch2(x)
        branch3 = self.branch3(x)
        branch4 = self.branch4(x)

        return torch.cat([branch1, branch2, branch3, branch4], 1)
```

Integrating Inception Modules into GoogLeNet

GoogLeNet consists of multiple Inception Modules, interspersed with convolutional, pooling, and fully connected layers.

```
class GoogLeNet(nn.Module):
    def __init__(self):
        super(GoogLeNet, self).__init__()
        self.conv1 = nn.Conv2d(1, 64, kernel_size=7, stride=2, padding=3)
        self.inception1 = InceptionModule(64)
        self.inception2 = InceptionModule(88)
        # Continue with further layers and Inception Modules

    def forward(self, x):
        x = self.conv1(x)
        x = self.inception1(x)
        x = self.inception2(x)
        # Continue with further layers and Inception Modules
        return x
```

Training and Evaluation

Training and evaluation of the GoogLeNet can be performed similarly to our previous CNN and simple neural network examples.

GoogLeNet's unique architecture and innovative Inception Modules represent an essential milestone in deep learning. By allowing the model to learn the optimal convolutions, the Inception Modules make the network more adaptable and capable of understanding complex patterns, all without a significant increase in computational cost.

Applying Image Augmentation on CIFAR-10

Image augmentation is an essential technique to expand the size and diversity of a training dataset by applying various transformations. These include rotations, flips, cropping, color adjustments, and more. By employing augmentation, a deep learning model can become more robust and generalized well on unseen data.

You will utilize PyTorch and torchvision libraries to apply image augmentation techniques to an image dataset. Specifically, you will use the CIFAR-10 dataset, a widely used dataset for image classification, containing 60,000 32x32 color images in 10 different classes.

Dataset Information

The CIFAR-10 dataset is available through the torchvision library, and can be found at below URL:
https://www.cs.toronto.edu/~kriz/cifar.html

Import Libraries

First, import the required libraries:

```
import torch
from torchvision import datasets, transforms
import matplotlib.pyplot as plt
```

Define Transformations

You will define a series of transformations to apply as augmentations. You will use random horizontal flips, random rotations, color jittering, and random cropping.

```
transform_augment = transforms.Compose([
    transforms.RandomHorizontalFlip(),
    transforms.RandomRotation(10),
    transforms.ColorJitter(brightness=0.2, contrast=0.2, saturation=0.2, hue=0.1),
    transforms.RandomResizedCrop(32, scale=(0.8, 1.0)),
    transforms.ToTensor()
])
```

Load CIFAR-10 Dataset with Augmentations

Next, we load the CIFAR-10 dataset and apply the defined augmentations.

```
train_dataset = datasets.CIFAR10(root='./data', train=True, download=True,
transform=transform_augment)
train_loader = torch.utils.data.DataLoader(train_dataset, batch_size=32, shuffle=True)
```

Visualize Augmented Images

To understand the impact of augmentations, you will visualize some examples.

```
def imshow(img):
    img = img / 2 + 0.5  # unnormalize
    plt.imshow(img.permute(1, 2, 0))
    plt.show()

# Retrieve a batch of training images
dataiter = iter(train_loader)
images, labels = dataiter.next()

# Display the first image
imshow(images[0])
```

This code will display an augmented image, and you can observe the effects of the applied transformations.

Integrate with Model Training

When training a CNN, such as the previously learned GoogLeNet, you can simply use this augmented dataset in the training loop. This will ensure that the model sees diverse variations of the training images, enhancing generalization.

Advantages and Considerations

Image augmentation has several benefits:

- Diversity: It introduces variations that enable the model to learn more generalized features.

- Overfitting Reduction: By artificially expanding the dataset, augmentation helps in reducing overfitting.

- Robustness: The model becomes more robust to slight changes and distortions in the input images.

However, it's essential to choose the augmentations that make sense for the specific problem. Over-augmenting the dataset with irrelevant transformations might lead to confusion rather than improvement. By applying these transformations, the model's performance can be significantly enhanced without the need for additional data collection. PyTorch and torchvision make it straightforward to apply various augmentations and integrate them into the training process.

Performing Object Detection on COCO

Object detection is a computer vision task that involves not only identifying objects within images but also providing a bounding box to locate where the object is in the image. In this segment, you will work with PyTorch to build an object detection model using a pre-trained model from the torchvision library. You will use the same CIFAR-10 dataset, but since it doesn't come with bounding box annotations, you will utilize a dataset specifically designed for object detection, such as the COCO dataset.

Dataset Information

The Common Objects in Context (COCO) dataset is one of the widely used datasets for object detection. It provides detailed annotations including object categories and bounding box coordinates. The dataset can be found at the below URL: https://cocodataset.org/

Import Libraries

Start by importing the necessary libraries:

```
import torch
import torchvision
from torchvision.models.detection import fasterrcnn_resnet50_fpn
from torchvision import datasets, transforms
from PIL import Image, ImageDraw
```

Define Transformations

You will define transformations to resize and convert images to tensors:

```
transform = transforms.Compose([
    transforms.ToPILImage(),
    transforms.Resize((800, 800)),
    transforms.ToTensor()
])
```

Load COCO Dataset

Load the COCO dataset with the torchvision library, applying the defined transformations:

```
coco_train = datasets.CocoDetection(root='./data/train',
annFile='./annotations/instances_train2017.json', transform=transform)
train_loader = torch.utils.data.DataLoader(coco_train, batch_size=2, shuffle=True)
```

Load Pre-Trained Model

You will use a pre-trained Faster R-CNN model, specifically tailored for object detection:

```
model = fasterrcnn_resnet50_fpn(pretrained=True)
model.eval()  # Set the model in evaluation mode
```

Perform Object Detection

With the model and dataset loaded, we can now run object detection on an example:

```
# Retrieve a batch of training images and annotations
images, targets = next(iter(train_loader))

# Perform prediction
with torch.no_grad():
    prediction = model(images)

# Get the first prediction
pred = prediction[0]

# Draw bounding boxes
image_with_boxes = Image.fromarray(images[0].mul(255).permute(1, 2,
0).byte().numpy())
draw = ImageDraw.Draw(image_with_boxes)

for element in range(len(pred['labels'])):
    boxes = pred['boxes'][element].cpu().numpy().astype(int)
    draw.rectangle(boxes, outline ="red")

image_with_boxes.show()
```

This code will display the image with bounding boxes around detected objects.

Explanation of Faster R-CNN

Faster R-CNN is one of the most popular architectures for object detection. It consists of two main parts:

- Region Proposal Network (RPN): It suggests possible object locations (proposals) in the image.
- Fast R-CNN: It uses the proposals from the RPN to accurately classify the objects and refine the bounding boxes.

The pre-trained Faster R-CNN model from torchvision has been trained on a large dataset like COCO, and it's capable of detecting multiple object categories.

The object detection model we built here can be applied to various applications like surveillance, autonomous driving, robotics, and more. By adjusting the architecture and fine-tuning the model on specific datasets, you can achieve high accuracy on specialized object detection tasks.

To incorporate object detection into previous examples such as the CNN or image augmentation techniques, you would need to adapt the dataset to include bounding box annotations or select a dataset specifically designed for object detection.

Perform Semantic Segmentation

Semantic segmentation is the task of classifying each pixel in an image into a specific class or category. It provides a comprehensive understanding of an image by depicting not only the objects present but also the pixels that constitute them. Continuing with our exploration in PyTorch, you will use a pre-trained model from the torchvision library to perform semantic segmentation on an image from the COCO dataset, which we previously used for object detection.

Import Libraries and Load Dataset

You will begin by importing necessary libraries and loading the dataset:

```
import torch
import torchvision
from torchvision import models, transforms
import matplotlib.pyplot as plt
from PIL import Image
```

Define Transformations

You will define transformations to preprocess the image:

```
preprocess = transforms.Compose([
    transforms.ToTensor(),
    transforms.Normalize(mean=[0.485, 0.456, 0.406], std=[0.229, 0.224, 0.225]),
])
```

Load Pre-Trained Model

PyTorch's torchvision library provides a DeepLabV3 model pretrained on a subset of COCO train2017:

```
model = models.segmentation.deeplabv3_resnet101(pretrained=True)
model.eval()
```

Process an Image

You will select an image from the previous example and preprocess it:

```
input_image = Image.open("path/to/your/image.jpg")
input_tensor = preprocess(input_image)
input_batch = input_tensor.unsqueeze(0)
```

Perform Segmentation

Now you will apply the model to the input image:

```
with torch.no_grad():
    output = model(input_batch)['out'][0]
```

Interpret the Output

The output is a tensor where each pixel corresponds to a particular class score. We can convert these scores into class labels:

```
output_predictions = output.argmax(0)
```

Visualization

To visualize the segmented image, you can map the class labels to specific colors. Following is a way to do that:

```
# Define the color mapping
palette = torch.tensor([2 ** 25 - 1, 2 ** 15 - 1, 2 ** 21 - 1])
colors = torch.as_tensor([i for i in range(21)])[:, None] * palette
colors = (colors % 255).numpy().astype("uint8")

# Map the labels to colors
r = Image.fromarray(output_predictions.byte().cpu().numpy()).resize(input_image.size)
r.putpalette(colors)

# Overlay the segmentation on the original image
seg_image = Image.blend(input_image, r.convert("RGB"), alpha=0.5)

plt.imshow(seg_image)
plt.show()
```

Understanding DeepLabV3

Overview

DeepLabV3 is a prominent model in the field of computer vision, specifically focusing on the task of semantic segmentation. Semantic segmentation is the process of classifying each pixel in an image into a predefined class. Unlike image classification where the entire image is assigned a single label, or object detection where bounding boxes are predicted around objects, semantic segmentation aims to provide a label for each individual pixel.

Key Features of DeepLabV3

- Dilated Convolutions: Traditional convolutional layers may lose some spatial information. Dilated convolutions allow the model to expand its receptive field without increasing the number of parameters. This is particularly useful for capturing fine-grained details in images.

- Atrous Spatial Pyramid Pooling (ASPP): This is a technique that probes an incoming feature map at multiple scales and then aggregates the outputs. It enables the model to capture objects and features at various scales in an image.

How Dilated Convolutions Work?

In a standard convolution operation, adjacent pixels are combined in a local receptive field. However, in dilated convolutions, the receptive field is expanded by introducing gaps (or "dilations") between the pixels in each convolutional filter. This enables the model to capture information from a larger area of the input image without increasing the number of parameters.

Imagine an image of a cat sitting on a mat. In a standard convolution operation, you might capture the details of the fur or whiskers. With dilated convolutions, you can capture those fine details while also taking into account larger features like the entire body of the cat or the mat it's sitting on.

Exploring Filters and Feature Maps

Filters and Feature Maps are core components of Convolutional Neural Networks (CNNs), which are widely used in various applications of computer vision. These elements play a critical role in enabling CNNs to recognize intricate patterns and features within an image. Let us delve into the mechanics of Filters and Feature Maps and demonstrate their functionality through PyTorch, while keeping in mind our ongoing example of medical imaging, particularly MRI scans of the brain.

Filters

Filters, often called convolutional kernels, are small matrices filled with learnable parameters. These matrices slide over the input image during the convolution operation. Different filters are responsible for detecting different features like edges, corners, or textures. For example, a filter could be specialized in recognizing the outlines of brain structures in an MRI scan. In most CNN architectures, multiple filters are employed. When you have multiple filters, you can detect multiple features, making the network more powerful and versatile.

Feature Maps

A Feature Map is essentially a matrix that is produced when a filter is convolved with an image. It indicates areas in the image where the corresponding feature (like an edge or a corner) has been detected. When multiple filters are applied to an image, a set of feature maps is generated. Each feature map represents the presence of a different feature in the image. In the context of a brain MRI, one feature map might highlight the boundaries of the cerebral cortex while another might focus on ventricular structures.

Sample Program: Using Filters and Feature Maps

Let us create a simple CNN with PyTorch and analyze the filters and feature maps.

Import Libraries and Load an Image

```
import torch
import torchvision.transforms as transforms
from torch import nn
import matplotlib.pyplot as plt
from PIL import Image

# Load and preprocess the image
image_path = "path/to/your/image.jpg"
image = Image.open(image_path)
transform = transforms.Compose([transforms.ToTensor()])
image_tensor = transform(image).unsqueeze(0)
```

Define Convolutional Layer

We will define a convolutional layer with a single filter.

```
conv_layer = nn.Conv2d(in_channels=3, out_channels=1, kernel_size=3)
```

Apply Convolutional Layer

Let us apply this layer to our image and visualize the Feature Map.

```
feature_map = conv_layer(image_tensor)
plt.imshow(feature_map[0, 0].detach().numpy(), cmap='gray')
plt.show()
```

Analyze the Filter

The weights of the filter can be accessed and visualized.

```
filter_weights = conv_layer.weight.data
plt.imshow(filter_weights[0, 0].detach().numpy(), cmap='gray')
plt.show()
```

Multiple Filters

We can define multiple filters by changing the out_channels parameter, and the resulting feature maps will show different detected features.

```
conv_layer_multiple = nn.Conv2d(in_channels=3, out_channels=6, kernel_size=3)
feature_maps_multiple = conv_layer_multiple(image_tensor)

# Visualizing the feature maps
for i in range(6):
    plt.subplot(2, 3, i+1)
    plt.imshow(feature_maps_multiple[0, i].detach().numpy(), cmap='gray')
plt.show()
```

The above explanation and code can be integrated with previous examples, including the CNN architecture we built or GoogleLeNet. The filters and feature maps at different layers of those networks could be visualized to understand what features the network is learning at various stages. The concept of filters and feature maps is not unique to CNNs but extends to more complex architectures like ResNet, VGG, etc. By analyzing the filters, we can gain insight into what the network is learning, which helps in debugging, improving, or interpreting the model. By unraveling the workings of filters and feature maps within CNNs, we gain a deeper understanding of how these models operate.

Building Time Series Model

Time series modeling involves analyzing sequences of data points ordered by time, often used in forecasting future values. In this sample program, you will create a time series model using PyTorch with a Long Short-Term Memory (LSTM) network, a type of recurrent neural network suitable for handling sequential data.

Selecting Dataset

You will be using the "Airline Passengers" dataset, a classic time series dataset containing monthly totals of international airline passengers from 1949 to 1960.

The dataset is available at the following URL:
https://raw.githubusercontent.com/jbrownlee/Datasets/master/airline-passengers.csv

Importing Libraries and Loading the Dataset

```
import torch
import torch.nn as nn
import pandas as pd
import numpy as np
import matplotlib.pyplot as plt

# Load the dataset
url = "https://raw.githubusercontent.com/jbrownlee/Datasets/master/airline-passengers.csv"
dataframe = pd.read_csv(url, usecols=[1])
dataset = dataframe.values
dataset = dataset.astype('float32')
```

Preprocessing Data

For time series data, we must normalize the values and create sequences for training the model.

```
from sklearn.preprocessing import MinMaxScaler
from torch.utils.data import TensorDataset, DataLoader

# Normalize the dataset
scaler = MinMaxScaler(feature_range=(0, 1))
dataset = scaler.fit_transform(dataset)

# Create sequences
look_back = 3
X, y = [], []
for i in range(len(dataset)-look_back-1):
    a = dataset[i:(i+look_back), 0]
    X.append(a)
```

```
    y.append(dataset[i + look_back, 0])

X = np.array(X)
y = np.array(y)

# Convert to PyTorch tensors
X_tensor = torch.tensor(X).float()
y_tensor = torch.tensor(y).float()

# Create DataLoader
dataset = TensorDataset(X_tensor, y_tensor)
dataloader = DataLoader(dataset, batch_size=1)
```

Defining Model

You will use an LSTM model with one hidden layer.

```
class TimeSeriesModel(nn.Module):
    def __init__(self, input_dim, hidden_dim):
        super(TimeSeriesModel, self).__init__()
        self.lstm = nn.LSTM(input_dim, hidden_dim)
        self.linear = nn.Linear(hidden_dim, 1)

    def forward(self, x):
        x, _ = self.lstm(x.view(len(x), 1, -1))
        x = self.linear(x.view(len(x), -1))
        return x
model = TimeSeriesModel(input_dim=look_back, hidden_dim=10)
loss_function = nn.MSELoss()
optimizer = torch.optim.Adam(model.parameters(), lr=0.01)
```

Training Model

```
epochs = 100
```

```
for epoch in range(epochs):
    for seq, labels in dataloader:
        optimizer.zero_grad()
        y_pred = model(seq)
        loss = loss_function(y_pred.view(-1), labels)
        loss.backward()
        optimizer.step()

print("Training completed.")
```

Making Predictions

```
# Predictions
test_inputs = torch.tensor(X[-look_back:]).float()
test_outputs = model(test_inputs)
predicted = scaler.inverse_transform(test_outputs.detach().numpy())
```

Visualization

You can visualize the results using Matplotlib.

```
plt.plot(dataset)
plt.plot(np.concatenate([dataset[:-len(predicted)], predicted]))
plt.show()
```

PyTorch requires the user to complete a number of essential steps in order to construct a time series model. These steps include preprocessing the data into a sequential format, defining an LSTM model that is suited for dealing with time series data, and training the model. You will be able to investigate time series analysis and gain a better understanding of how these models function in practice if you apply this method to the "Airline Passengers" dataset.

Common Challenges & Solutions

When working with Convolutional Neural Networks (CNNs), image processing, and time series modeling in PyTorch, as we have in this chapter, several potential errors may arise. Let us explore these errors and provide practical solutions.

Mismatched Input and Filter Dimensions

When you're building a CNN for image classification, you need to specify parameters like kernel size, stride, and padding for the convolutional layers. If these parameters are not set correctly, the dimensions of the output may not match what you expect, leading to errors.

Let us consider you're working with grayscale images of size 28×28×28×28. You decide to use a kernel of size 5×5×5×5 with a stride of 2 and no padding.

```
import torch
import torch.nn as nn

input_image = torch.randn(1, 1, 28, 28)  # Batch size of 1, 1 channel, 28x28 image
conv_layer = nn.Conv2d(1, 32, kernel_size=5, stride=2, padding=0)
```

When you try to perform the convolution, you might run into dimensionality issues.

Solution - To address this, you should make sure that the dimensions of your input, kernel, stride, and padding are compatible. The formula to calculate the output size

$$O = \frac{N - K + 2P}{S} + 1$$

```
import torch.nn.functional as F

output = F.conv2d(input_image, conv_layer.weight, stride=2, padding=0)
```

Using this formula can help verify the dimensions before implementation. You can also use PyTorch's functional API, which can automatically handle some of these issues for you.

GPU Memory Error

When you're running deep learning models, you might encounter GPU memory errors, especially with large datasets or complex network architectures.

Continuing with our image classification task, let us consider you're using a very deep CNN and a large batch size.

```
input_images = torch.randn(1024, 1, 28, 28).cuda() # Large batch size
```

Solution - Following are some strategies to avoid running into GPU memory errors:

- Reduce Batch Size: Smaller batches require less memory but might lead to a less stable gradient descent.

```
input_images = torch.randn(256, 1, 28, 28).cuda() # Reduced batch size
```

- Memory-efficient Architecture: Use architectures that are designed to be more memory-efficient, like MobileNets.

- Mixed-Precision Training: PyTorch's AMP (Automatic Mixed Precision) can reduce memory usage and speed up computation.

```
from torch.cuda.amp import autocast, GradScaler

scaler = GradScaler()

with autocast():
    output = model(input_images)
    loss = criterion(output, labels)

scaler.scale(loss).backward()
scaler.step(optimizer)
scaler.update()
```

Overfitting

Overfitting occurs when the model learns the training data too well, including its noise and outliers, and fails to generalize to unseen data. In our customer churn example, an overfit model might perform exceptionally well on the dataset it was trained on but fail miserably when exposed to new customer data.

Solution -

- Regularization Techniques: Techniques like dropout and weight decay can be applied to the model. Dropout randomly sets a fraction of input units to 0 during training, which can help in preventing overfitting. Weight decay (L2 regularization) adds a penalty term to the loss function, discouraging the model from fitting to the noise in the training set.

- Early Stopping: During training, monitor the model's performance on a validation set. Stop training as soon as the validation loss stops improving, even if the training loss continues to decrease.

- Data Augmentation: In the context of our customer churn model, data augmentation might involve creating synthetic data that mimics the behavior of actual customers. This increases the diversity of the training data and helps improve generalization.

Difficulty in Convergence (Optimization)

The model's loss might remain constant or even increase during training, indicating the model is having difficulty converging. In the customer churn scenario, this could mean that despite many training epochs, the model isn't getting better at predicting which customers will churn.

Solution -

- Adjust the Learning Rate: A too high or too low learning rate can hinder convergence. Experiment with different values or employ learning rate annealing strategies.

- Adaptive Learning Rate Techniques: Algorithms like Adam adjust the learning rate during training, which can often help with convergence.

- Normalize Input Data: Ensuring that all features have the same scale can make the optimization landscape smoother, aiding in faster and more stable convergence.

- Weight Initialization: Properly initializing the network weights can also accelerate convergence. Methods like He or Xavier initialization are commonly used.

Incompatible Data Types

Mismatched data types, such as float32 and float64, can lead to errors during training. In our telecom example, this could occur if the customer usage data is in float64 while the model's weights are in float32.

Solution -

- Uniform Data Types: Before training, ensure that the input data and model weights are of the same data type.
- Use .to(device): This method can be used to ensure that all tensors (input data, model weights, etc.) are on the appropriate computation device, be it CPU or GPU.

Errors with Time Series Data

Time series data is often collected over an extended period and can have a variety of issues such as missing values, outliers, or inconsistencies. These can severely impact the performance of predictive models like ARIMA, LSTM, or Prophet, which rely on historical data to forecast future values.

Solution -

- Handling Missing Values: There are several ways to handle missing values in time series data.
- Imputation: You can impute missing values using statistical methods like mean, median, or even using interpolation techniques.
- Backfill or Forward Fill: Values can be filled using the previous or the next available data point.
- Normalization: Time series data can often have varying scales. Normalization techniques like Min-Max Scaling or Z-Score normalization can be applied to bring all the variables to a common scale, improving numerical stability.

Image Augmentation Issues

Image augmentation is crucial for increasing the dataset size and improving model generalization. However, incorrect augmentations like extreme rotations, zoom, or color changes can distort the image beyond recognition, resulting in poor model performance.

Solution -

- Use Standard Libraries: Libraries like torchvision.transforms offer a variety of pre-implemented, well-tested image augmentation techniques that are generally safe to use.
- Test Augmentations: Before applying any augmentation techniques on the entire dataset, it's essential to test them on sample images to ensure they don't distort the data.

Object Detection and Semantic Segmentation Errors

In object detection and semantic segmentation, the quality of the bounding boxes, annotations, and segmentation masks is crucial. Errors in these areas can mislead the model during the training process.

Solution -

- Validate Annotations: It's essential to validate the format and consistency of the annotations. For example, ensure that the coordinates of bounding boxes are within the image dimensions.
- Standard Datasets: Using reputable, well-annotated datasets like COCO or Pascal VOC can help ensure quality. If you're using custom datasets, rigorous pre-processing and validation are crucial.

Custom Layers Implementation Mistakes

When you're creating custom layers for your sentiment analysis model, mistakes like incorrect tensor dimensions or incompatible activation functions can result in unexpected model behavior.

Solution -

- Read PyTorch Guidelines: Familiarize yourself with PyTorch's guidelines for creating custom layers.
- Isolation Testing: Before incorporating the custom layer into your main model, test it independently using a smaller set of data. For instance, in our NLP project, you can test your custom layer with a few example sentences to ensure it's working as expected.

Dataset URL Errors

If you're pulling a dataset of customer reviews from an online source, you might encounter broken URLs or permission issues that prevent dataset access.

Solution -

- URL Validation: Before implementing it in your code, make sure to validate the URL by accessing it through a browser.
- Manual Download: If automatic downloading fails, manually download the dataset and read it into your NLP project.

Model Serialization with TorchScript

When you try to convert your sentiment analysis model to TorchScript format, you might face compatibility issues. This is often because certain PyTorch functionalities are not supported in TorchScript.

Solution -

- Compatibility Check: Do verify all layers and operations in your model are TorchScript-compatible.
- Consult Documentation: Always consult the official PyTorch documentation for the most accurate and up-to-date procedures for converting your model.

CUDA Compatibility Issues

In our NLP project, you may want to use CUDA for faster computations. However, if CUDA is not properly installed or configured, you might encounter errors.

Solution -

- Version Check: Do verify that the CUDA version installed is compatible with the version of PyTorch you are using.
- Availability Check: Run torch.cuda.is_available() in your code to ensure that CUDA is available for use. If this returns False, there's likely an issue with your CUDA setup.

You will be able to navigate the challenges that may arise when working with CNNs, time series modeling, and other related tasks in PyTorch if you first identify and understand the potential errors that may occur, as well as the solutions that correspond to those errors.

Summary

We began our investigation of convolutional neural networks (CNNs) in this chapter by gaining an understanding of both their theoretical underpinnings and the significance of their application. We covered fundamental ideas such as kernel sizes, filters, and pooling layers as we dove into the construction of a basic CNN from a practical standpoint. In addition, the implementation of Google LeNet architecture in practical settings gave us the opportunity to investigate an effective real-world deep learning model. Image preprocessing is an essential component of modern computer vision tasks, and the introduction of image augmentation techniques and their application to an open-source dataset provided hands-on experience with the technique.

The application of PyTorch libraries allowed us to recognise various objects contained within images as we continued our exploration of practical applications. In addition to that, we dove into semantic segmentation and investigated different ways to assign a particular category to each pixel in an image. The study of Filters and Feature Maps, which are fundamental to having an understanding of how CNNs capture spatial hierarchies in data, served as a supplement to both of these exercises. PyTorch's versatility was demonstrated by the fact that it was not only used to model image data, but also sequential data, such as stock prices and weather patterns. Time Series modeling was another aspect that was investigated.

Overall, we learned a variety of difficulties and mistakes that one might make while working with these concepts. We learned a variety of practical solutions to overcome these challenges, ranging from dimension mismatches and GPU memory problems to overfitting and incorrect data types. In the areas of image augmentation, object detection, semantic segmentation, and time series modeling, we paid particular attention to the challenges that are unique to their respective domains. This hands-on approach to troubleshooting and problem-solving equips you with the tools necessary to build robust and efficient deep learning models in PyTorch. This not only includes the creation of complex systems but also their refinement and optimisation.

CHAPTER 4: RECURRENT NEURAL NETWORKS

Recurrent Neural Networks Overview

Recurrent Neural Networks (RNNs) are a class of artificial neural networks designed to recognise patterns in sequences of data such as text, genomes, handwriting, spoken language, and numerical time series data. RNNs are also known as convolutional neural networks. In contrast to feedforward neural networks, recurrent neural networks (RNNs) have connections that loop backward. This enables information to persist, which is an essential quality for comprehending sequences and lists.

The concept of sequential memory, in which information can be passed on from one step of the sequence to the next, is the central idea that underpins RNNs. When performing tasks that require an understanding of the context and order, having this connection between previous and subsequent data points is essential.

RNNs have become increasingly important in Natural Language Processing (NLP), particularly with regard to translation, speech recognition, and opinion mining. RNNs are a good fit for the sequential nature of language, which allows them to perform well. To generate a sentence that makes sense or to translate one language into another, for instance, requires not only an understanding of individual words but also of the context in which those words are used and the order in which those words are used. The field of finance makes use of RNNs for forecasting stock prices, foreign exchange rates, and other time-dependent financial metrics. They have the ability to recognise patterns and trends over extended periods of time, which contributes to more accurate forecasting. RNNs have also found uses in the field of healthcare, particularly in the area of predictive diagnostics. They are able to anticipate the progression of diseases or the likelihood of particular medical events by conducting an analysis of sequential data such as patient history and vital signs.

Traditional RNNs have some shortcomings, despite the fact that they have some advantages, such as having difficulty learning long-range dependencies within sequences. This issue prompted the development of advanced RNN structures, such as networks with Long Short-Term Memory (LSTM) and Gated Recurrent Units (GRU), which mitigate this problem. RNNs have a tremendous amount of untapped potential in terms of potential future applications. The need to understand sequential data in various fields and to make predictions based on this data is only going to increase as this type of data continues to proliferate rapidly. RNNs are likely to play an important role in shaping the future of deep learning and artificial intelligence, whether it be in autonomous driving, where sequential sensor data needs to be analyzed, or in personalized healthcare, where ongoing patient monitoring can lead to timely interventions. This is the case regardless of whether the application is in autonomous driving or personalized healthcare.

Data Preparation for LSTM

Long Short-Term Memory networks, also known as LSTM networks, are one subcategory of recurrent neural networks. These networks are able to learn long-term dependencies in sequence data. In order to guarantee that the model is able to recognise the underlying patterns in the sequence, it is necessary to take a number of essential steps when preparing the data for LSTM models. The following is a demonstration of how to practically prepare data.

Choosing the Dataset and Objective

In this sample program, you will focus on working with a time series dataset. Specifically, you will employ daily weather data for our examples and analyses. Time series data is particularly fascinating because it allows us to analyze patterns over a chronological sequence, making it ideal for predictions and trend analysis.

The primary objective of this exercise is to develop a predictive model for forecasting next day's temperature based on historical weather observations. This would involve techniques such as data preprocessing, feature selection, and employing machine learning algorithms tailored for time series data.

For the purpose of this program, the daily weather data can be downloaded from a source labeled as "Weather Data." and can be found in the below URL: https://github.com/jbrownlee/Datasets/blob/master/daily-min-temperatures.csv

Loading and Inspecting Data

In the first step of your data analysis journey, you'll want to get your data into a format that is easy to manipulate. One of the most efficient ways to do this is by loading your dataset into a Pandas DataFrame. You may externally refer to a tutorial available in the below URL: https://practicaldatascience.co.uk/data-science/how-to-import-data-into-pandas-dataframes

By doing so, you gain the ability to perform a wide range of operations, from simple data transformations to complex queries, with minimal code. Once the data is loaded, it's crucial to get a sense of what the data looks like and what it contains. To achieve this, you can preview the initial rows using methods like df.head(). Additionally, it's beneficial to generate a statistical summary using df.describe() to understand the data's distribution, central tendency, and spread.

Data Preprocessing

Missing values can introduce bias or lead to incorrect conclusions. There are multiple techniques to address this, such as imputation—where you fill in missing values based on other observations—or simply removing the rows or columns with missing data. When working with algorithms sensitive to the scale of input features, like Long Short-Term Memory networks (LSTMs), scaling becomes vital. Two common scaling methods are normalization and standardization. Normalization rescales features to a range of [0,1], while standardization transforms them to have a mean of 0 and standard deviation of 1.

Transforming Data into Sequences

In time-series analysis or sequence prediction tasks, windowing is a common technique. This involves creating a "sliding window" of consecutive data points (lag observations) as input variables to predict the subsequent value in a sequence. The length of the sequence you choose can affect the model's performance. Select a sequence length that aligns well with the underlying patterns in your data and is suitable for the specific prediction task you're tackling.

Splitting Data into Training and Test Sets

The method you select for splitting your dataset into training and test sets can vary based on the problem you're solving. For problems where sequence integrity is crucial, a sequential split is advisable. Alternatively, for problems where individual data points are independent, a random split may suffice.

Reshaping Data for LSTM Input

LSTM expects input data to be a 3D array of shape (samples, time steps, features). Reshape your data accordingly.

Following is a sample code snippet to walk you through these steps:

```
import pandas as pd
from sklearn.preprocessing import MinMaxScaler
from sklearn.model_selection import train_test_split

# Load data
url = "https://github.com/jbrownlee/Datasets/blob/master/daily-min-
temperatures.csv"
data = pd.read_csv(url)

# Preprocess
scaler = MinMaxScaler()
data['temperature'] = scaler.fit_transform(data[['temperature']])

# Transform to sequences
sequence_length = 10
sequences = []
```

```
for i in range(len(data) - sequence_length):
    seq = data['temperature'].iloc[i:i+sequence_length+1].values
    sequences.append(seq)

# Split
X, y = [seq[:-1] for seq in sequences], [seq[-1] for seq in sequences]
X_train, X_test, y_train, y_test = train_test_split(X, y, test_size=0.2)

# Reshape
X_train = np.array(X_train).reshape((len(X_train), sequence_length, 1))
X_test = np.array(X_test).reshape((len(X_test), sequence_length, 1))
```

Following these steps will prepare your data in the required format, at which point you will be able to feed it into an LSTM model in order to train it. Your particular problem and the characteristics of your data should inform your decision regarding the appropriate sequence length, scaling method, and other preprocessing steps.

Building LSTM Model

Building an LSTM (Long Short-Term Memory) model requires understanding the sequential nature of the data, as well as carefully constructing the architecture to capture underlying patterns. Below, you will go through the process of constructing an LSTM model using PyTorch, which builds on the data preparation steps from the previous section.

Importing Required Libraries

First, you'll need to import PyTorch and other required libraries:

```
import torch
import torch.nn as nn
import torch.optim as optim
```

Defining LSTM Model Class

Create a class that defines your LSTM architecture. This involves specifying the number of layers, hidden units, and other parameters that define how the LSTM will be constructed.

```
class LSTMModel(nn.Module):
    def __init__(self, input_dim, hidden_dim, batch_size, output_dim=1, num_layers=2):
        super(LSTMModel, self).__init__()
        self.input_dim = input_dim
        self.hidden_dim = hidden_dim
        self.batch_size = batch_size
        self.num_layers = num_layers

        # Define the LSTM layer
        self.lstm = nn.LSTM(self.input_dim, self.hidden_dim, self.num_layers)

        # Define the output layer
        self.linear = nn.Linear(self.hidden_dim, output_dim)

    def init_hidden(self):
        # Initialize hidden and cell states
        return (torch.zeros(self.num_layers, self.batch_size, self.hidden_dim),
                torch.zeros(self.num_layers, self.batch_size, self.hidden_dim))

    def forward(self, input):
        # Forward pass through LSTM layer
        lstm_out, self.hidden = self.lstm(input.view(len(input), self.batch_size, -1),
self.hidden)

        # Only take the output from the final timestep
        y_pred = self.linear(lstm_out[-1].view(self.batch_size, -1))
        return y_pred.view(-1)
```

Instantiating Model

Create an instance of the LSTM class, specifying the parameters that suit your specific problem:

```
input_dim = 1  # input dimension
hidden_dim = 64  # hidden layer dimension
```

```
batch_size = 16  # batch size
model = LSTMModel(input_dim=input_dim, hidden_dim=hidden_dim,
batch_size=batch_size)
```

Defining Loss Function and Optimizer

Select a suitable loss function and an optimizer for training the model:

```
loss_function = nn.MSELoss()  # Mean Squared Error Loss
optimizer = optim.Adam(model.parameters(), lr=0.01)  # Adam optimizer
```

Training LSTM Model

The training loop involves iterating through batches of data, performing forward and backward passes, and updating the weights.

```
epochs = 100
for epoch in range(epochs):
    for i in range(len(X_train)//batch_size):
        # Get batch
        batch_X = torch.tensor(X_train[i*batch_size : (i+1)*batch_size],
dtype=torch.float32)
        batch_y = torch.tensor(y_train[i*batch_size : (i+1)*batch_size],
dtype=torch.float32)

        # Initialize hidden state
        model.hidden = model.init_hidden()

        # Zero gradients
        optimizer.zero_grad()

        # Forward pass
        y_pred = model(batch_X)

        # Compute loss
```

```
loss = loss_function(y_pred, batch_y)

# Perform backpropagation
loss.backward()

# Update weights
optimizer.step()
```

This piece of code provides an overview of the typical steps involved in defining, instantiating, and training an LSTM model by utilizing PyTorch. It is important to fine-tune the hyperparameters, such as hidden_dim, batch_size, epochs, and learning rate, so that they are appropriate for the data and problem at hand. In the following steps, you will be able to evaluate the model, give it additional adjustments, and, if necessary, make predictions.

Exploring Gated Recurrent Units (GRU)

Introduction to GRU and LSTM

Gated Recurrent Units (GRUs) and Long Short-Term Memory (LSTM) units are specialized types of Recurrent Neural Network (RNN) architectures that play a pivotal role in the processing of sequential or time-series data. While they both serve similar overarching purposes, they have distinct characteristics that can influence their effectiveness in various applications. In this exploration, we delve into the theoretical foundations of GRUs and LSTMs to better understand their similarities, differences, and optimal use-cases.

A primary challenge in training traditional RNNs is the vanishing gradient problem. This issue arises when gradients—values used during the training process to update the model's weights—become exceedingly small. As a result, the RNN struggles to learn from information in earlier time steps, which is often critical for tasks like language modeling, sequence prediction, and time-series forecasting.

Both GRUs and LSTMs were engineered to address this very problem. They incorporate specialized gating mechanisms that allow for the selective flow of information, making it easier for the network to remember or forget certain details. This enhances their ability to capture long-term dependencies in the data.

Architecture Differences: LSTM vs. GRU

LSTM: A Four-Component Architecture

- Input Gate: In LSTM networks, the input gate plays a crucial role in deciding which pieces of incoming information are valuable and should be stored in the cell state. This allows the LSTM to focus on the most relevant parts of the input for long-term retention.

- Forget Gate: This component decides which information from the cell state should be thrown away or 'forgotten.' By doing so, the LSTM can make room for new, more relevant information.

- Output Gate: The output gate of an LSTM scrutinizes the cell state and decides which information to send as output. This is particularly important when the network needs to make predictions or decisions based on the learned data.

- Cell State: Serving as the LSTM's memory, the cell state is a critical component that carries relevant information throughout the sequence of data. It acts like a conveyor belt, allowing important information to be passed along through the sequence.

GRU: A Simplified Yet Effective Architecture

- Reset Gate: The GRU employs a reset gate to determine how much of the past information should be forgotten. This is a simplified mechanism that combines aspects of LSTM forget and input gates.

- Update Gate: This gate is responsible for deciding the extent to which the current state should influence the hidden state and how much of the previous state should be carried forward. This allows the GRU to balance new and old information effectively.

- No Distinct Cell State: Unlike LSTMs, GRUs lack a separate cell state. Instead, the hidden state itself serves the purpose of carrying information through the time steps.

Computational Complexity

LSTMs, with their additional gate and distinct cell state, usually have a higher number of parameters and require more computational power. This often translates into increased training time and higher memory requirements.

GRUs are generally more lightweight due to their simplified architecture. This can be advantageous when computational resources are limited or when quick model training is a priority.

Learning Capabilities

LSTMs are considered more expressive due to their complex structure, potentially leading to better performance in capturing long-term dependencies. However, this is not universally true

and depends on the specific task and dataset.
GRUs, with their simplified structure, may train faster and require fewer resources. They might be preferred when you have a constrained computational budget or when the task doesn't require complex long-term dependency modeling.

Empirical Performance

In the real world, the decision between using an LSTM or a GRU is often based on empirical evidence. It's common to experiment with both architectures on your specific task and dataset, then compare their performances on a validation set. This approach allows you to select the most effective architecture for your particular application.

The choice between GRU and LSTM is nuanced and highly dependent on the specific problem, dataset, and constraints of the project. While LSTMs offer a more complex and potentially powerful model, GRUs provide a more streamlined and computationally efficient alternative. Experimentation is key, and understanding the underlying mechanics of both models will help in selecting the most appropriate architecture for a given task.

Building GRU Model

Now that we have a solid grasp of the theoretical underpinnings of GRUs, let us move on to the next step, which is to construct a GRU model utilizing the data that we had previously prepared for the LSTM. In order to build, test, and evaluate the GRU model, you will utilize the PyTorch framework and proceed in a methodical, step-by-step fashion. In order to maintain coherence throughout the learning process, you will keep making use of the same data and activities as before.

Importing Libraries and Loading Data

Since the data preparation steps were previously completed, you will continue using the same dataset. Assuming that the data is split into training and validation sets and preprocessed, we can start by importing the necessary PyTorch libraries.

```
import torch
import torch.nn as nn
from torch.autograd import Variable
import torch.optim as optim
```

Defining GRU Model

You will create a GRU model with one or more GRU layers. Following is a simple program with one layer:

```
class GRUModel(nn.Module):
    def __init__(self, input_dim, hidden_dim, layer_dim, output_dim):
        super(GRUModel, self).__init__()
        self.hidden_dim = hidden_dim
        self.layer_dim = layer_dim
        self.gru = nn.GRU(input_dim, hidden_dim, layer_dim, batch_first=True)
        self.fc = nn.Linear(hidden_dim, output_dim)

    def forward(self, x):
        h0 = Variable(torch.zeros(self.layer_dim, x.size(0), self.hidden_dim))
        out, _ = self.gru(x, h0)
        out = self.fc(out[:, -1, :])
        return out
```

Setting Hyperparameters

Defining the hyperparameters such as input dimension, hidden layer dimension, output dimension, learning rate, etc.

```
input_dim = 10
hidden_dim = 32
layer_dim = 1
output_dim = 1
learning_rate = 0.01
```

Creating Model

Instantiating the GRU model and defining the loss function and optimizer.

```
model = GRUModel(input_dim, hidden_dim, layer_dim, output_dim)
loss_function = nn.MSELoss() # Depending on your task, this might change
optimizer = optim.Adam(model.parameters(), lr=learning_rate)
```

Training Model

You will use the same training loop as the one used previously for the LSTM.

```
epochs = 100
for epoch in range(epochs):
    # Forward pass
    outputs = model(train_data)
    optimizer.zero_grad()

    # Compute loss
    loss = loss_function(outputs, train_labels)

    # Backward pass
    loss.backward()
    optimizer.step()
```

Evaluation

You can evaluate the model using the validation set by running the forward pass and comparing the predictions with the actual values.

```
model.eval()
test_outputs = model(validation_data)
# Compute validation metrics as required
```

This demonstration offers a step-by-step instruction manual for developing a GRU model with PyTorch. You will be able to successfully train a GRU for the particular task and dataset you provide if you follow the steps. As was mentioned in the previous section, one can see the benefits of using GRU rather than LSTM when it comes to the amount of time and resources that are required for training. You will be able to further enhance the performance of the model by playing around with the various hyperparameters.

Understanding Sequential Modeling

What is Sequential Modeling?

Sequential modeling is a specialized form of data modeling that focuses on the order and relationship between individual data points in a sequence. Unlike other types of modeling where data points are often considered independent, sequential modeling understands that the order of observations can carry significant meaning. Whether it's predicting stock prices, generating text, or understanding audio signals, the essence of sequential modeling lies in its ability to capture temporal or sequential patterns within the data.

In many real-world applications, data does not exist in isolation. For instance, in natural language processing, the order of words in a sentence is crucial for understanding its meaning. Similarly, in time-series forecasting, like weather prediction, the data points are chronologically ordered, and each observation is often correlated with its preceding and succeeding points. Ignoring the sequence could lead to a loss of valuable contextual information and, consequently, less accurate or meaningful models.

Applications of Sequential Modeling

- Time-Series Forecasting: One of the most prevalent uses of sequential modeling is in the fields of finance and economics, where predicting future data points based on historical patterns can be invaluable. For example, predicting stock prices or economic indicators relies heavily on understanding past trends.

- Natural Language Processing (NLP): Sequential models are indispensable in NLP tasks. Whether it's generating coherent text, translating languages, or analyzing sentiment, the order of words is crucial for accurate results.

- Music and Video Analysis: In creative domains like music and video, sequential modeling can analyze and understand the arrangement of musical notes or the sequence of frames. This can be useful in tasks like automated music composition or video summarization.

- Medical Diagnostics: In healthcare, tracking a patient's vital signs over a period can provide insights into their health. Sequential modeling can help in predicting potential health risks based on these temporal patterns.

- Robotics and Control Systems: In automated systems, understanding the sequence of actions to accomplish a task is essential. Sequential models can optimize these actions, making robots and control systems more efficient.

- Anomaly Detection: Recognizing abnormal patterns in data is another vital application. In scenarios like fraud detection or network security, understanding the typical data sequence helps in identifying anomalies effectively.

Sample Program: Building Sequence Model

Given the data prepared previously, you will walk through the unique steps to build a sequence model using PyTorch. You will skip the common parts already taught in previous chapters or sections.

Choosing Appropriate Model

Depending on the task, you might choose LSTM, GRU, Transformer, or other sequential models. Let us assume we're using LSTM for this particular program.

Structuring Model Architecture

While we have already learned LSTM creation, in a sequential task, you may want to combine LSTM with other layers like convolutional layers for a more complex structure.

```
class SequenceModel(nn.Module):
    def __init__(self):
        super(SequenceModel, self).__init__()
        self.lstm = nn.LSTM(input_dim, hidden_dim, layer_dim, batch_first=True)
        self.conv1 = nn.Conv1d(hidden_dim, conv_dim, kernel_size)
        self.fc = nn.Linear(conv_dim, output_dim)

    def forward(self, x):
        out, _ = self.lstm(x)
        out = self.conv1(out)
        out = self.fc(out[:, -1, :])
        return out
```

Sequence-Specific Preprocessing

Your data might need reshaping or other transformations specific to sequential tasks. For example, you might use sliding windows to create sequences from time-series data.

Advanced Training Techniques

Considering sequential dependencies, techniques like Teacher Forcing in sequence-to-sequence models could be applied.

Interpretation and Evaluation

Understanding how the model is making sequential predictions might require specialized visualization or evaluation metrics, such as BLEU score for text translation tasks.

In order to build a sequence model, one must first understand the particular requirements of the sequential data and the sequential task. In order to successfully model sequential relationships, it is essential to combine sequential models with other neural network components, specialized preprocessing, training techniques, and evaluation methods. This particular demonstration extends our ongoing journey of continuous learning by providing an overview of the theory and practical considerations necessary to successfully build and apply a sequence model to the previously prepared data.

Sample Program: Time Series Analysis using LSTM

Building a time series analysis model involves processing sequential data to understand underlying temporal patterns and predict future values. Since we have previously learned LSTM and GRU models, let us now explore how to apply these to time series analysis, specifically focusing on the dataset and examples we have previously worked with.

You will use the LSTM model in this demonstration, as it is widely used in time series forecasting due to its ability to capture long-term dependencies. Assuming we're using the dataset prepared earlier, ensure that the data represents a sequential pattern, such as stock prices, weather data, or any time-bound information.

Preprocessing and Structuring Data

When dealing with time-series data, specialized preprocessing techniques are often required to prepare the data for LSTM (Long Short-Term Memory) models. This is crucial for the model to effectively learn the underlying temporal patterns and make accurate predictions.

Following are the key steps involved:

Scaling Data Through Normalization

Normalizing your time-series data is often the first preprocessing step when preparing it for LSTM models. This involves scaling the data features so that they fall within a specific range, commonly between 0 and 1. Normalization helps in stabilizing the training process, as it ensures that no particular feature disproportionately impacts the model's learning.

Segmenting Data using Windowing Techniques

After scaling the data, the next task is to divide it into manageable "windows" or "segments" that the LSTM model can ingest. Depending on the specific requirements of your project, these windows can either overlap or be mutually exclusive. The size of the window is another critical parameter to decide upon, as it can significantly affect the model's ability to capture long-term or short-term trends.

Data Partitioning

Finally, it's essential to split your preprocessed data into distinct sets for training, validation, and testing. The training set is used to adjust the model's parameters, while the validation set helps in tuning hyperparameters and gives an indication of the model's performance. The testing set is reserved for evaluating how well your model will perform on unseen data.

```
from sklearn.preprocessing import MinMaxScaler

scaler = MinMaxScaler()
data_normalized = scaler.fit_transform(data)

def create_sequences(data, seq_length):
    sequences = []
    for i in range(len(data) - seq_length):
        seq = data[i: i + seq_length]
        sequences.append(seq)
    return torch.tensor(sequences)

seq_length = 10
data_sequences = create_sequences(data_normalized, seq_length)
```

Building LSTM Model

Create the LSTM architecture with an appropriate number of layers, hidden dimensions, and output dimensions specific to the time series task.

```
class TimeSeriesModel(nn.Module):
    def __init__(self):
        super(TimeSeriesModel, self).__init__()
```

```
        self.lstm = nn.LSTM(input_size, hidden_size, num_layers, batch_first=True)
        self.fc = nn.Linear(hidden_size, output_size)

    def forward(self, x):
        out, _ = self.lstm(x)
        out = self.fc(out[:, -1, :])
        return out
```

Training Model

Define loss function, optimizer, and train the model using the prepared sequences.

```
model = TimeSeriesModel()
criterion = nn.MSELoss()
optimizer = torch.optim.Adam(model.parameters(), lr=learning_rate)

for epoch in range(num_epochs):
    outputs = model(data_sequences[:, :-1])
    optimizer.zero_grad()
    loss = criterion(outputs, data_sequences[:, -1])
    loss.backward()
    optimizer.step()
```

Making Predictions and Evaluation

Use the trained model to make predictions on the test set. Evaluate the model using appropriate metrics such as Mean Squared Error (MSE) or Mean Absolute Error (MAE). Analysis of time series using LSTM necessitates the use of particular preprocessing methods, as well as design and training considerations for the model architecture. We will be able to construct a reliable model for forecasting time series if we apply these to the dataset and examples that came before.

Creating Multi-layer RNN

Incorporating a multi-layer Recurrent Neural Network (RNN) into your machine learning pipeline can offer significant advantages, particularly when dealing with intricate sequential data. A multi-layer RNN is essentially a stack of RNN layers where the output of one layer serves as the input for the next. This architecture enhances the model's capability to capture more complex, high-level temporal representations in the data.

Designing Model Architecture

Continuing with the time-series analysis example we learned earlier, let us consider the prospect of implementing a multi-layer RNN using PyTorch. PyTorch provides a flexible and dynamic computational graph, making it an excellent choice for building sophisticated RNN models. You can easily extend a single-layer RNN to a multi-layer one by adjusting the 'num_layers' parameter when defining your RNN layer in PyTorch. This addition can make your model more adept at understanding nuanced temporal relationships, thereby potentially improving its predictive performance. Adding multiple layers can, however, increase the computational complexity, both in terms of memory and processing time. It's essential to balance the trade-off between model complexity and computational efficiency. You'll also want to pay attention to the risk of overfitting, especially if your dataset is not large enough to justify the added complexity.

Following is how we can define a multi-layer LSTM in PyTorch:

```
class MultiLayerRNN(nn.Module):
    def __init__(self, input_size, hidden_size, output_size, num_layers):
        super(MultiLayerRNN, self).__init__()
        self.lstm = nn.LSTM(input_size, hidden_size, num_layers, batch_first=True)
        self.fc = nn.Linear(hidden_size, output_size)

    def forward(self, x):
        h_0 = torch.zeros(num_layers, x.size(0), hidden_size)  # Initial hidden state
        c_0 = torch.zeros(num_layers, x.size(0), hidden_size)  # Initial cell state
        out, _ = self.lstm(x, (h_0, c_0))
        out = self.fc(out[:, -1, :])
        return out
```

Preparing Data

You will continue using the same time series data prepared in the previous section.

Training Multi-layer RNN

The training process remains similar to the single-layer RNN. Instantiate the model with the desired number of layers and follow the same training loop:

```
num_layers = 3
model = MultiLayerRNN(input_size, hidden_size, output_size, num_layers)

optimizer = torch.optim.Adam(model.parameters(), lr=learning_rate)
criterion = nn.MSELoss()

for epoch in range(num_epochs):
    outputs = model(data_sequences[:, :-1])
    loss = criterion(outputs, data_sequences[:, -1])
    optimizer.zero_grad()
    loss.backward()
    optimizer.step()
```

Evaluation and Predictions

Evaluate the model using the same metrics and visualization techniques as before. Following are some of the considerations to be taken into account:

- Complexity: Adding more layers increases the model's complexity, potentially leading to overfitting.
- Training Time: More layers mean more parameters, so training can be slower.
- Hyperparameter Tuning: The number of layers is a hyperparameter that you may want to optimize.

Creating a multi-layer RNN enhances the model's ability to capture complex relationships. By building upon the previous example, we've explored how to practically design, train, and evaluate a multi-layer RNN in PyTorch. By extending our time series analysis with this architecture, we have gained hands-on experience with a powerful and commonly used structure in sequential modeling.

Common Challenges & Solutions

In building RNNs, particularly complex structures like multi-layer RNNs, LSTM, and GRU, several potential issues and errors may arise. Understanding these problems and knowing how to tackle them is crucial for successful model implementation. Below, you will examine some of the common challenges and how to resolve them:

Vanishing and Exploding Gradients Problem

In deep learning models like RNNs, as the gradients are back-propagated, they can start to vanish (approach zero) or explode (grow very large) in deep networks. This problem becomes particularly pronounced in networks with long sequences, which is a common scenario for RNNs for below reasons:

- As the gradient becomes infinitesimally small, weight updates during the training process become negligible, causing learning to stall or stop. This primarily occurs because the gradient values multiplied many times during backpropagation tend to approach zero, especially if the gradient is small (less than 1).

- Opposite to vanishing, the gradients in this case grow exponentially as they're propagated backward through each layer. This can cause weight values to become extremely large, leading to an unstable network.

Solution -

- Gradient Clipping: When the gradients are back-propagated, they are checked against a threshold. If they exceed this threshold, they're clipped or scaled down to keep them within a manageable range and prevent them from exploding.

- Proper Initialization: Methods like Xavier (or Glorot) initialization and He initialization are designed to set the initial weights of the neural network to values that prevent the gradient problem. Xavier initialization is more suitable for sigmoid and tanh activation functions, while He initialization works best for ReLU activations.

- Using Activation Functions: Non-linear activation functions like ReLU and its variants (like Leaky ReLU) help in preventing the vanishing gradient problem. The Leaky ReLU allows a small gradient when the unit is not active, thus ensuring some gradient even for inactive paths in the network.

Overfitting Problem

Overfitting occurs when a model learns the training data too closely, including its noise and outliers, making it perform poorly on unseen or new data. It captures the specificities of the training data and fails to generalize, leading to high accuracy on training data but low accuracy on test data.

Solutions -

- Dropout: During training, randomly selected neurons are ignored, or "dropped-out". This ensures that the network doesn't rely too heavily on any specific neuron, promoting generalization.

- L2 Regularization (or weight decay): It adds a penalty to the loss function for large weights. The penalty is proportional to the sum of the squared weights, discouraging the model from fitting too closely to the training data.

- Early Stopping: As the model trains, both training and validation errors are monitored. Even though the training error might keep decreasing, there comes a point when the validation error stops decreasing and may start to increase. This indicates the point where the model starts to overfit, and training can be stopped. This strategy, thus, helps in preventing overfitting by stopping the training process before the model starts to over-train.

Difficulty in Learning Long-term Dependencies

Traditional Recurrent Neural Networks (RNNs) have an inherent shortcoming: their inability to capture and learn long-term dependencies in a sequence. This is because the memory in RNNs, while iterative and recurrent, can fade or get diluted over longer sequences. Consequently, they might remember recent information but forget earlier data points. This limitation hampers their ability to model intricate relationships in sequences where the context from prior steps is crucial.

Solution -

- Attention mechanisms revolutionized sequence-to-sequence tasks by enabling the model to "focus" on different parts of the input sequence when producing an output. Rather than relying solely on the final hidden state of an RNN, attention allows the model to weigh input states across a sequence, emphasizing the most relevant parts at each step. This strategy is particularly effective for tasks like machine translation, where the importance of different words in the source sequence can vary depending on the target translation.

Computational Cost and Training Time

As the architecture of neural networks, particularly RNNs, becomes more profound and intricate, the number of parameters to be trained can explode. This increased complexity, while allowing the capture of more nuanced patterns, comes with a significant computational cost. Training these heavy models requires more memory and leads to extended training times, often demanding specialized hardware.

Solutions -

- Instead of updating the model's weights after every single data point (stochastic gradient descent), batch training involves updating weights after a group or "batch" of data points. This approach can make more efficient use of computational resources by leveraging vectorized operations.

- Mini-batch gradient descent, a middle-ground between full batch and stochastic gradient descent, strikes a balance by updating weights after a subset of the training data, optimizing both speed and convergence properties.

- Graphics Processing Units (GPUs) are designed to handle parallel operations, making them ideal for the matrix and tensor operations found in deep learning. Moving model training to a GPU can lead to a significant reduction in training time. Modern deep learning frameworks like PyTorch and TensorFlow have GPU integration, allowing for seamless shifting between CPU and GPU.

- For extraordinarily large models or datasets, even a single GPU might not suffice. In such cases, distributed training can be employed. This involves splitting the training process across multiple GPUs or even across different machines. Techniques like gradient accumulation ensure that the model remains consistent across these multiple training nodes.

Sequence Length Variability

Sequences in datasets often vary in length. When feeding them into recurrent neural networks (RNNs) that expect fixed-length input, this variability can create issues.

Solutions -

- To handle sequences of different lengths, padding can be applied. By adding zeros or other specified values to the shorter sequences, they can be made to match the length of the longest sequence in the dataset.

- While padding can adjust sequence lengths, it introduces non-informative values. Using masking allows the model to ignore these padded values during computation, ensuring that they don't adversely affect the training or prediction process.

Model Complexity and Selection

Selecting the right architecture for an RNN model involves making decisions about the type of RNN to use, the number of layers, the number of hidden units, and other parameters. With numerous combinations possible, identifying the optimal configuration is complex.

Solutions -

- Rather than manually selecting hyperparameters, employ techniques like grid search and random search. These methods systematically explore various combinations to identify the set that delivers the best performance.

- To objectively assess the performance of different model architectures, utilize cross-validation techniques. This involves partitioning the dataset into multiple subsets to validate the model's robustness. Complement this with metrics that offer insights into model accuracy, loss, and other relevant parameters.

Data Preprocessing Issues

The quality of a model's output is heavily reliant on the quality of its input. Mistakes in data preprocessing, like inconsistent scaling or misaligned sequences, can substantially impair model performance.

Solutions -

- Scaling transforms data values to fall within a specific range. It's vital to ensure consistency in this transformation. When both training and testing datasets undergo scaling, they must be scaled using the same method and parameters to maintain data integrity.

- When dealing with time-series data or any sequential data, ensuring proper alignment is crucial. This involves arranging sequences in a way that aligns corresponding data points correctly, especially when sequences have missing or out-of-order values. Proper alignment ensures that the model receives accurate and meaningful input.

Deep learning practitioners can more effectively navigate the complexities of RNNs if they have a solid understanding of these potential pitfalls and put the practical solutions listed to use. These guidelines provide a robust framework for developing, training, and deploying RNNs within a variety of applications and domains. Some examples of RNNs include LSTM models and GRU models. We can ensure that the implementation will go more smoothly and that the results will be more reliable if we anticipate these challenges and employ these strategies.

Summary

The chapter's investigation of Recurrent Neural Networks (RNNs) shed light on a variety of RNNs and their applications, such as LSTM (Long Short-Term Memory) and GRU (Gated Recurrent Units). It was demonstrated how complicated the process of preparing data for LSTM models can be, with a particular focus on the significance of accurate scaling and sequence alignment. In this chapter, practical guidelines for creating LSTM, GRU models, and multi-layer RNNs were presented, revealing how these models are suited for sequential modeling and time-series analysis.

The theoretical teaching on RNNs was supported by practical demonstrations that highlighted their current applications in deep learning and AI areas, as well as their potential applications in the future. In the chapter, GRU was contrasted with LSTM to illustrate why the former may be preferred. This comparison helped shed light on GRU's capacity to more effectively capture long-term dependencies in sequences. The practical applications have been expanded to include time-series modeling, as well as the creation of multi-layer RNNs, which highlights their adaptability to a variety of different complex modeling tasks.

The chapter also addressed potential errors and issues that could arise when working with RNNs, and it provided comprehensive solutions to deal with these problems. Practical solutions were outlined for each of the challenges, ranging from the issue of vanishing and exploding gradients to the challenge of overfitting and variability in sequence length. The comprehensive analysis and troubleshooting solutions not only deepened the reader's understanding of RNNs but also provided them with the tools and information they required to successfully apply this understanding in a variety of real-world settings.

CHAPTER 5: NATURAL LANGUAGE PROCESSING

Role of PyTorch in Natural Language Processing

PyTorch has become a cornerstone in the field of Natural Language Processing (NLP) due to its flexibility, user-friendly interface, and robust capabilities. Because of these characteristics, it is ideally suited to meet the intricate and constantly changing requirements of NLP projects. It is equipped with the ability to support a wide variety of pre-trained models, including BERT, GPT, and Transformer, all of which have shown their worth in applications such as text classification, machine translation, summarization, and question answering.

PyTorch's support for dynamic computation graphs is one of the features that really sets it apart from other similar tools. This is especially helpful in applications for natural language processing (NLP) where the length of sentences can vary, necessitating that the model architecture adjust dynamically. PyTorch's dynamic nature, on the other hand, makes the process of coding and debugging more intuitive than it is with frameworks that use static computation graphs. Both newcomers and seasoned programmers can benefit tremendously from the support provided by PyTorch's comprehensive documentation, which is accompanied by a multitude of tutorials and a lively community forum. Because of this, a thriving ecosystem has been established that is consistently pushing the limits of what is possible in the field of NLP.

PyTorch is extremely versatile in terms of the applications it can be used for. Its neural networks are highly effective in sentiment analysis, which is a technique that is frequently applied in consumer product reviews and in market research. PyTorch has also made significant contributions to the field of machine translation, particularly with the advent of deep learning models such as Seq2Seq. It supports both extractive and abstractive text summarization methods, both of which are helpful in the process of information retrieval. In addition, the use of its specialized architectures, such as Recurrent Neural Networks (RNNs), is making it easier to develop applications that convert speech to text.

In the realm of creativity, generative models such as GPT and LSTM have been put to use for a variety of text generation tasks, ranging from the composition of poetry to that of narratives. Advanced question-answering systems have also been made possible thanks to the development of PyTorch's Transformer and attention mechanisms. PyTorch is making strides in healthcare by assisting in the extraction of insights from complex medical texts, which in turn helps in the prediction of disease and the recommendation of treatment. These applications are outside of the realm of general applications. Additionally, it is becoming increasingly popular for use in the construction of industry-specific chatbots in a variety of fields, including customer service and entertainment, among others.

Preprocessing Textual Data

Text preprocessing is a critical step in most NLP tasks. It involves cleaning and transforming raw text data into a format that can be fed into a machine learning model. TorchText is a package in PyTorch that offers tools to make working with text data easier. Let us walk through a practical example of preprocessing text data using TorchText.

Importing Libraries

First, you will need to import TorchText and other essential libraries.

```
import torchtext
from torchtext.data import Field, TabularDataset, Iterator
```

You can use the IMDB dataset, which is a popular open-source dataset for sentiment analysis.

```
from torchtext.datasets import IMDB
```

Defining Fields

Fields define how the data should be processed. We will create a TEXT field for the review and a LABEL field for the sentiment.

```
TEXT = Field(tokenize='spacy', lower=True, batch_first=True)
LABEL = Field(sequential=False, use_vocab=False, batch_first=True)
```

Loading Dataset

Load the IMDB dataset, specifying the fields.

```
train_data, test_data = IMDB.splits(TEXT, LABEL)
```

Building Vocabulary

You need to build a vocabulary for the TEXT field from the training dataset. This will convert words into integers.

```
TEXT.build_vocab(train_data, max_size=10000, vectors="glove.6B.100d")
```

In the above snippet, we limit the vocabulary to 10,000 words and use GloVe embeddings.

Creating Iterators

Iterators will allow you to loop through the dataset in batches.

```
train_iterator, test_iterator = Iterator.splits(
    (train_data, test_data),
    batch_size=64,
    device='cuda' # or 'cpu'
)
```

Accessing Batch

You can now access a batch of data by iterating over the training iterator.

```
for batch in train_iterator:
    text = batch.text # The tokenized, integer-encoded text
    label = batch.label # The corresponding labels
    Break
```

Additional Preprocessing

You can further preprocess the text data as required, including handling stopwords, stemming, or any domain-specific cleaning.

After going through this particular demonstration, you should now be familiar with how to use TorchText to preprocess the IMDB dataset. You have developed a vocabulary, loaded the dataset, crafted iterators, and accessed a batch of data. You have additionally loaded the dataset and defined the fields. Because it provides a method that is both effective and streamlined for managing common text preprocessing responsibilities, TorchText gives you the ability to concentrate on developing and training your natural language processing (NLP) models.

Building Text Classification Model

Building a text classification model in PyTorch involves defining the model architecture, training it on the preprocessed data, and evaluating its performance. Continuing from the previous example, you will now create a text classification model to predict the sentiment of movie reviews from the IMDB dataset.

Define Model Architecture

You will create a simple LSTM model for text classification.

```
import torch.nn as nn

class TextClassifier(nn.Module):
    def __init__(self, vocab_size, embedding_dim, hidden_dim, output_dim, n_layers,
dropout):
        super(TextClassifier, self).__init__()

        # Embedding layer
        self.embedding = nn.Embedding(vocab_size, embedding_dim)

        # LSTM layer
        self.lstm = nn.LSTM(embedding_dim, hidden_dim, n_layers, dropout=dropout,
batch_first=True)

        # Fully connected layer
        self.fc = nn.Linear(hidden_dim, output_dim)

        # Dropout layer
        self.dropout = nn.Dropout(dropout)

    def forward(self, text):
        embedded = self.embedding(text)
        lstm_out, _ = self.lstm(embedded)
        lstm_out = self.dropout(lstm_out[:, -1, :])
        output = self.fc(lstm_out)
        return output
```

Initialize Model

You will initialize the model with the appropriate dimensions and transfer it to the GPU if available.

```
vocab_size = len(TEXT.vocab)
embedding_dim = 100
hidden_dim = 256
output_dim = 1
n_layers = 2
dropout = 0.5

model = TextClassifier(vocab_size, embedding_dim, hidden_dim, output_dim, n_layers,
dropout)
model.to('cuda' if torch.cuda.is_available() else 'cpu')
```

Loss and Optimizer

You will use the Binary Cross-Entropy Loss with Adam optimizer.

```
import torch.optim as optim

criterion = nn.BCEWithLogitsLoss()
optimizer = optim.Adam(model.parameters(), lr=0.001)
```

Training Model

You will train the model using the previously created iterator.

```
model.train()
num_epochs = 10

for epoch in range(num_epochs):
    for batch in train_iterator:
        text, label = batch.text, batch.label
        optimizer.zero_grad()
        predictions = model(text).squeeze(1)
        loss = criterion(predictions, label.float())
        loss.backward()
        optimizer.step()
```

Evaluating Model

You will define a function to evaluate the model on the test data.

```
def evaluate(model, iterator, criterion):
    model.eval()
    total_loss = 0

    with torch.no_grad():
        for batch in iterator:
            text, label = batch.text, batch.label
            predictions = model(text).squeeze(1)
            loss = criterion(predictions, label.float())
            total_loss += loss.item()

    return total_loss / len(iterator)


test_loss = evaluate(model, test_iterator, criterion)
print(f"Test Loss: {test_loss}")
```

Building on the understanding you gained from preprocessing the IMDB dataset, this sample demonstration has shown you how to create a straightforward LSTM text classification model using PyTorch. You began by defining the architecture of the model, then you initialized it. After that, you selected a loss function and an optimizer. Finally, you trained the model using the training data, and then you tested it using the test data. You can improve performance by fine-tuning the hyperparameters further, adding additional layers, or experimenting with different architectural approaches.

Building Seq2Seq Model

Building a sequence-to-sequence (seq2seq) model for machine translation using PyTorch is an exciting application of deep learning. In this sample demonstration, you will transform our previous text classification model into a machine translation model that can translate English sentences into another language, such as French.

Loading the Dataset

You will use the Multi30k dataset for translation from English to German. TorchText provides an easy way to download and preprocess this dataset.

```
from torchtext.data.utils import get_tokenizer
from torchtext.datasets import Multi30k
from torchtext.vocab import build_vocab_from_iterator

SRC_LANGUAGE = 'de'
TGT_LANGUAGE = 'en'

# Define Tokenizers
token_transform = {}
token_transform[SRC_LANGUAGE] = get_tokenizer('spacy', language='de')
token_transform[TGT_LANGUAGE] = get_tokenizer('spacy', language='en')

# Yield tokenized source and target sentences
def yield_tokens(data_iter, language):
    language_index = {SRC_LANGUAGE: 0, TGT_LANGUAGE: 1}
    for data_sample in data_iter:
        yield token_transform[language](data_sample[language_index[language]])

# Build Vocabulary
vocab_transform = {}
for ln in [SRC_LANGUAGE, TGT_LANGUAGE]:
    train_iter = Multi30k(split='train', language_pair=(SRC_LANGUAGE,
TGT_LANGUAGE))
    vocab_transform[ln] = build_vocab_from_iterator(yield_tokens(train_iter, ln),
min_freq=1)
```

Defining Encoder

The encoder will process the input sequence and compress the information into a context vector.

```
class Encoder(nn.Module):
    def __init__(self, input_dim, emb_dim, hidden_dim, n_layers, dropout):
        super(Encoder, self).__init__()
```

```
        self.embedding = nn.Embedding(input_dim, emb_dim)
        self.rnn = nn.LSTM(emb_dim, hidden_dim, n_layers, dropout=dropout)
        self.dropout = nn.Dropout(dropout)

    def forward(self, src):
        embedded = self.dropout(self.embedding(src))
        outputs, (hidden, cell) = self.rnn(embedded)
        return hidden, cell
```

Defining Decoder

The decoder will take the context vector and generate the translated sequence.

```
class Decoder(nn.Module):
    def __init__(self, output_dim, emb_dim, hidden_dim, n_layers, dropout):
        super(Decoder, self).__init__()
        self.embedding = nn.Embedding(output_dim, emb_dim)
        self.rnn = nn.LSTM(emb_dim, hidden_dim, n_layers, dropout=dropout)
        self.fc_out = nn.Linear(hidden_dim, output_dim)
        self.dropout = nn.Dropout(dropout)

    def forward(self, input, hidden, cell):
        input = input.unsqueeze(0)
        embedded = self.dropout(self.embedding(input))
        output, (hidden, cell) = self.rnn(embedded, (hidden, cell))
        prediction = self.fc_out(output.squeeze(0))
        return prediction, hidden, cell
```

Combining Encoder and Decoder

You will combine the encoder and decoder into a Seq2Seq model.

```
class Seq2Seq(nn.Module):
    def __init__(self, encoder, decoder, device):
        super(Seq2Seq, self).__init__()
```

```
        self.encoder = encoder
        self.decoder = decoder
        self.device = device

    def forward(self, src, trg, teacher_forcing_ratio=0.5):
        # ... Implementation of forward pass ...
```

Training the Model

The training loop is similar to the previous example but adapted for the seq2seq structure.

Inference

For inference, we need to write a separate loop that takes the encoder's hidden and cell states and decodes the target sequence one token at a time.

```
def translate_sentence(sentence, src_vocab, trg_vocab, model, device, max_length=50):
    # ... Implementation of translation ...
```

In this practical example, we have explored the architecture of a sequence-to-sequence model for machine translation using PyTorch. We began with the Multi30k dataset, defined an encoder and decoder using LSTM layers, combined them into a seq2seq model, trained the model, and wrote an inference function to translate new sentences. This basic architecture can be further enhanced with attention mechanisms, more sophisticated tokenization, and additional training techniques.

Building Transformers

Transformers have emerged as a formidable architecture in the realm of natural language processing, spearheading groundbreaking progress across a plethora of applications. Their prowess lies in the ability to grasp long-range sequence dependencies, a feature particularly useful in challenges like language translation. To elucidate, let us first demystify the concept of transformers and then walk through the construction of a transformer model for language translation—translating English to German—using PyTorch.

Introduction to Transformers

The seminal paper "Attention is All You Need" by Vaswani and colleagues in 2017 first presented transformers. Unlike LSTM-based sequence-to-sequence models, transformers employ an architecture that is divided into an Encoder and a Decoder, with the spotlight on self-attention mechanisms. The self-attention mechanism empowers the transformer model to prioritize different parts of the input sequence while constructing the output. This is orchestrated through the query, key, and value (Q, K, V) representations that are derived from the input data. The Encoder and Decoder in a transformer model aren't monolithic; they are constructed from several identical layers, often six. Each of these layers is bifurcated into two principal components: a multi-head self-attention unit and a position-wise feed-forward neural network.

Building Transformer Model

Preparing Data

You will stick to the Multi30k dataset that we used in our previous example to ensure consistency and comparability.

Defining Model

One of the standout features in a transformer model is positional encoding, which infuses the sequence of tokens with information about their respective positions. This enables the model to incorporate the order of tokens, a crucial aspect when dealing with sequences.

```
class PositionalEncoding(nn.Module):
    def __init__(self, d_model, dropout=0.1, max_len=5000):
        super(PositionalEncoding, self).__init__()
        # ... Implementation of positional encoding ...
```

Using the in-built nn.Transformer module, we can define the transformer model.

```
class TransformerModel(nn.Module):
    def __init__(self, ntoken, ninp, nhead, nhid, nlayers, dropout=0.5):
        super(TransformerModel, self).__init__()
        self.model_type = 'Transformer'
        self.pos_encoder = PositionalEncoding(ninp, dropout)
        self.encoder = nn.Embedding(ntoken, ninp)
        self.ninp = ninp
        self.transformer = nn.Transformer(ninp, nhead, nlayers, nhid, dropout)
        self.decoder = nn.Linear(ninp, ntoken)
        self.init_weights()

    def init_weights(self):
```

```
        # ... Initialization of weights ...

    def forward(self, src, tgt, src_mask, tgt_mask):
        # ... Implementation of forward pass ...
```

Training Model

Training the transformer model involves preparing the data, defining the model, and training it using the training loop. Attention masks can be used to prevent the model from looking at future tokens in the sequence.

Evaluation and Inference

The translation can be performed similarly to the seq2seq model but adapted for the transformer's architecture.

Building a transformer model using PyTorch for the English-German translation task involves defining the model's architecture, including the positional encoding and multi-head self-attention mechanism, training the model, and performing translations. The code provided above outlines the structure, and experimenting with different hyperparameters, layer configurations, and training strategies can further improve the model's performance.

Enhancing NER Model

Named Entity Recognition (NER) is a critical NLP task where the goal is to classify named entities in the text into predefined categories such as names of persons, organizations, locations, expressions of times, quantities, monetary values, percentages, etc. Improving existing NER models with PyTorch involves using state-of-the-art techniques and incorporating more complex architectures to enhance the model's performance. We will focus on these aspects in this section.

Assuming you have a baseline NER model built with a simple neural architecture like a BiLSTM, you might be leveraging word embeddings (like Word2Vec or GloVe) and character-level embeddings.

How about we see how to push this further.

Enhancing Word Representations

Using pre-trained models like BERT or RoBERTa that offer contextual word representations can add richer semantic information.

```
from transformers import BertTokenizer, BertModel

tokenizer = BertTokenizer.from_pretrained('bert-base-uncased')
model = BertModel.from_pretrained('bert-base-uncased')

inputs = tokenizer("Hello, my dog is cute", return_tensors="pt")
outputs = model(**inputs)
```

Adding More Layers

Adding CRF Layer

A Conditional Random Field (CRF) layer on top of the LSTM can help capture the structure in the output sequence and improve predictions.

```
import torch
import torch.nn as nn
from torchcrf import CRF

class BiLSTM_CRF(nn.Module):
    def __init__(self, vocab_size, tag_to_ix, embedding_dim, hidden_dim):
        super(BiLSTM_CRF, self).__init__()
        # ... LSTM layer code ...
        self.crf = CRF(len(tag_to_ix), batch_first=True)

    def forward(self, sentence, tags):
        # ... LSTM forward pass ...
        loss_value = -self.crf(emissions, tags, mask=mask)
        return loss_value
```

Model Training Enhancements

Hyperparameter Tuning

Fine-tuning hyperparameters like learning rate, batch size, and dropout rate can significantly impact the model's performance.

Advanced Optimization Techniques

Using advanced optimizers like AdamW and learning rate scheduling can improve convergence. Adding techniques like dropout, layer normalization, or even data augmentation can make your model more robust.

Continuous evaluation using metrics like Precision, Recall, and F1-score, and detailed error analysis can instruct model improvements.

Putting It All Together

The given below is a skeleton code that demonstrates how to combine these elements into a comprehensive model training routine:

```
class NER_Model(nn.Module):
    # Model Definition with CRF, LSTM layers

# Data Preparation
# ...

# Model, Loss, and Optimizer
model = NER_Model(vocab_size, tag_to_ix, embedding_dim, hidden_dim)
optimizer = torch.optim.AdamW(model.parameters(), lr=0.001)

# Training Loop
for epoch in range(epochs):
    for batch in dataloader:
        # Forward Pass
        loss = model(batch.text, batch.tags)

        # Backward Pass
        loss.backward()

        # Update
        optimizer.step()
        optimizer.zero_grad()
```

Experimentation and ongoing evaluation will assist you in honing in on the specific combination of strategies that will yield the best results. The combination of these components is what leads to the improvements, and that includes the application of pre-trained embeddings as well as advanced architectural components like CRF layers. Experiment with a variety of tactics and keep a close eye on the performance of your model at all times to guarantee that the adjustments are producing the desired outcomes.

NLP Pipeline Optimization

The optimization of natural language processing pipelines is a difficult task that requires a combination of strategies to ensure that the pipelines are effective, efficient, and scalable. Because of this optimization, your models will be able to train more quickly, will require less memory, and will in general be easier to manage.

The following is an in-depth practical example on how to optimize an NLP pipeline utilizing PyTorch, which can be applied to any of the earlier NLP models that we've developed:

Data Preprocessing Optimization

Parallelizing Data Loading

Utilize parallel processing for data loading and preprocessing. PyTorch's DataLoader allows you to set the number of parallel workers.

```
from torch.utils.data import DataLoader

dataloader = DataLoader(dataset, batch_size=32, shuffle=True, num_workers=4)
```

Efficient Tokenization and Padding

Use efficient tokenization libraries and only pad sequences to the maximum length in each batch rather than the entire dataset.

Model Architecture Optimization

Utilizing Efficient Layers and Operations

Replace traditional LSTM with quantized versions or use layers that have been optimized for specific hardware, such as NVIDIA's Tensor Cores.

Reducing Model Complexity

Pruning or reducing the size of the model by removing neurons, layers, or even using knowledge distillation can have a significant impact.

Training Optimization

Mixed Precision Training

Utilizing mixed precision (combining float16 with float32) can significantly speed up training without a noticeable loss in accuracy.

```
from torch.cuda.amp import autocast, GradScaler

scaler = GradScaler()

with autocast():
    output = model(input)
    loss = loss_fn(output, target)

scaler.scale(loss).backward()
scaler.step(optimizer)
scaler.update()
```

Gradient Accumulation

Accumulating gradients over several mini-batches allows you to effectively train with a larger batch size without increasing GPU memory requirements.

```
accumulation_steps = 4
loss = model(input, target)
loss = loss / accumulation_steps
loss.backward()

if (step+1) % accumulation_steps == 0:
    optimizer.step()
    optimizer.zero_grad()
```

Adaptive Learning Rate Scheduling

Methods like 1Cycle Policy or Cosine Annealing can adapt the learning rate during training, speeding up convergence.

Inference Optimization

Model Quantization

Quantizing the model can reduce the model size and make inference faster, especially on platforms with limited computational resources.

Batch Inference

Using batches during inference can help you leverage parallelism in the GPU, making predictions faster.

Optimizing Custom Layers

If you've implemented custom layers, ensure that they are as efficient as possible by utilizing optimized library functions wherever possible.

Utilizing Distributed Training

If your dataset is large, distributed training using tools like Horovod or PyTorch's native DistributedDataParallel can significantly reduce training times.

The process of optimizing an NLP pipeline involves a number of moving parts, and the strategy that proves to be the most successful will be determined by the particular needs of your model and data. Experimentation and careful analysis by making use of profiling tools are going to be your best instructor for determining which optimizations will yield the best results. Keep in mind that the goal is not simply to make things go more quickly; rather, it is to do so while simultaneously maintaining or even improving accuracy and robustness. Validate at regular intervals to ensure that your optimizations have not adversely affected the performance of your model.

Common Challenges & Solutions

In the domain of NLP and with the use of PyTorch, various errors might arise throughout the different stages of building models. The given below is an in-depth look at some potential errors and how to address them:

Data Preprocessing Errors

Incorrect Tokenization

Tokenization is the foundational step in text preprocessing where raw text is split into chunks, typically words or subwords. Incorrect tokenization can drastically affect downstream tasks such as translation, sentiment analysis, or information retrieval. Common pitfalls include splitting at wrong places or not recognizing certain compound words or phrases.

Solution - To resolve these issues, it's paramount to select the appropriate tokenization strategy aligned with the specifics of your language or the nuances of your task. Many languages have unique linguistic constructs, idiomatic expressions, or compound nouns that standard tokenizers might not handle optimally. Leveraging dedicated libraries such as HuggingFace's Tokenizers library can be extremely beneficial. This library provides pre-built tokenizers for numerous languages, and they're often trained on massive corpora ensuring broad coverage. Beyond this, manually inspecting the tokenized output on sample data and adjusting the tokenizer's rules, if necessary, can provide an additional layer of assurance.

Character Encoding Issues

In the era of globalization, data often comprises multilingual content with diverse scripts and special characters. Character encoding issues can manifest when reading data files without specifying the correct character set, leading to artifacts like 'mojibake' or garbled text. Especially non-Latin scripts, diacritical marks, or certain punctuation marks might not be rendered correctly, affecting the quality of your data and potentially the outcomes of any analysis or modeling.

Solution - Always ensure data consistency by setting a standard encoding type, preferably 'utf-8', across your pipeline when reading or writing files. 'utf-8' is a widely accepted encoding standard that can represent any character in the Unicode standard, making it suitable for multilingual datasets. Additionally, during the preprocessing phase, one might encounter specific special characters or sequences that need bespoke handling. Utilize text processing tools to identify, replace, or remove these anomalies. It's also beneficial to employ libraries like chardet in Python to automatically detect the character encoding of a file. Lastly, always inspect a subset of your data after loading to ensure characters are displayed as intended, allowing for timely identification and rectification of any encoding mishaps.

Model Architecture Errors

Mismatched Dimensions

A frequent stumbling block when assembling deep learning models is the incompatibility of dimensions between sequential layers. This inconsistency can halt the propagation of data through the model, causing an error. In a well-structured model, the output of one layer should seamlessly become the input for the subsequent layer. If there's a mismatch, PyTorch will flag it, often leading to confusion for newcomers.

Solution - Always be cognizant of the dimensions when adding layers to your model. PyTorch's error messages are particularly helpful in this scenario. They not only highlight the presence of an error but also provide detailed information about the expected and the provided sizes. By analyzing this, you can quickly locate the layer causing the discrepancy. Furthermore, using tools like tensor shape printing intermittently during model building can help keep track of dimensions and ensure consistent alignment.

Unsupported Input Types

Every layer in PyTorch expects inputs of a particular data type. Feeding it an unsupported type will lead to issues, inhibiting the model's functionality. When tensors of incorrect data types, like int64 instead of the commonly used float32, are passed to a model or a particular layer, PyTorch flags an error. This type misalignment can be due to various reasons - data loading methods, previous operations, or unintended typecasting.

Solution - Regularly verifying the data type of tensors, especially before passing them into the model, is crucial. If you encounter a type-related error, PyTorch's diagnostics will inform you of the expected data type. To address this, utilize the .to() method available for tensors. This method allows you to effortlessly convert tensor types. For instance, if a tensor x is of type int64 and you need it as float32, you can transform it using x.to(torch.float32). Establishing a practice of regularly checking and managing tensor types ensures smoother model operations and reduces the chances of unexpected issues.

Training Errors

Exploding or Vanishing Gradients

Gradients play a pivotal role in adjusting a model's weights. When training a deep neural network, gradients can sometimes either grow exponentially (exploding) or shrink down, becoming almost negligible (vanishing). Both situations can severely hamper the training process. The weights during the training process unexpectedly turn into NaN (Not a Number) or reach extremely high values tending towards infinity. A very high learning rate can make the model diverge, leading to exploding gradients. In very deep networks, especially those without normalization layers, gradients can vanish or explode as they are back propagated. Weights that are improperly initialized can exacerbate the problem of unstable gradients.

Solution -

- Adjust Learning Rate: Begin by using a smaller learning rate, or consider adaptive learning rate methods like Adam or AdaGrad which adjust the learning rate during training.

- Gradient Clipping: This technique sets a threshold value and rescales the gradients if they exceed this threshold, effectively controlling their explosion.

- Weight Initialization: Utilize techniques like He or Xavier initialization, which consider the size of the previous layer to determine an optimal weight initialization.

Overfitting

Overfitting occurs when a model learns the training data too well, including its noise and outliers, thereby reducing its ability to generalize to new, unseen data. The model exhibits stellar performance on training data but demonstrates a significant drop in performance on validation or test data. A model with excessive layers or neurons might become too adaptable, fitting even to the noise in the training data. Training on a small dataset can often lead to overfitting as the model might memorize rather than generalize. If training proceeds for an excessive number of epochs without any stopping criterion, the model might start overfitting.

Solution -

- Regularization: Techniques like L1 and L2 regularization add a penalty to the loss function, discouraging the model from assigning too much importance to any one feature.
- Dropout: It's a technique wherein random neurons are "dropped out" or turned off during training. This ensures that no single neuron or group becomes overly specialized.
- Increase Validation Set: Enlarge the validation dataset. This provides a larger set of unseen data against which the model's generalizing capacity can be tested.
- Early Stopping: Monitor the model's performance on the validation set and stop training once performance plateaus or starts to degrade, indicating the onset of overfitting.

Inference Errors

Out-of-Vocabulary Words

During the inference phase, models can sometimes encounter words that were not present in the training dataset. These words are termed as "out-of-vocabulary" (OOV) words. Such words can significantly affect the performance and accuracy of the model since it's unacquainted with these terms. For language models or natural language processing systems, handling OOV words is particularly crucial as languages are constantly evolving with the introduction of new terms, slang, and colloquialisms.

Solution -

- Subword Tokenization: One of the approaches to tackle OOV words is through subword tokenization. In this method, words are broken down into smaller units or subwords. For instance, the word 'unbelievable' might be tokenized into 'un-', 'believ-', and '-able'. This ensures that even if the entire word hasn't been seen by the model during training, the model recognizes the smaller units, allowing for more accurate predictions.

- Special Token for Unknown Words: Another commonly used technique is to introduce a special token, often denoted as <UNK>, to represent any word not available in the training vocabulary. During training, a fraction of words from the training data can be replaced with this <UNK> token. During inference, any OOV word is replaced with the <UNK> token, which the model has been trained to recognize and handle.

Inconsistent Preprocessing

Data preprocessing is a crucial step in preparing the data for training machine learning or deep learning models. It involves multiple operations like normalization, tokenization, and removal of stop words. If the data during the inference phase is not preprocessed in the same manner as the training data, it can lead to significant inconsistencies in the model's predictions. The model might not recognize certain patterns or features, leading to errors.

Solution -

- Standardize Preprocessing Pipeline: Create a standardized preprocessing pipeline that is used consistently across both training and inference. This pipeline should include every step, from data cleaning to feature extraction, ensuring that data fed during inference undergoes the exact same transformation as the training data.

- Use Configuration Files: Save all preprocessing parameters, like tokenization rules, normalization constants, and vocabulary lists, in configuration files or scripts. These can be referred to or loaded during inference, ensuring that the exact same parameters are applied.

- Automate Preprocessing: To minimize human errors and inconsistencies, automate the preprocessing steps as much as possible. This can be achieved by creating a dedicated preprocessing function or module, which can be called during both training and inference.

Optimization Errors

Non-Convergence

During the training phase, the model fails to converge, meaning that the loss doesn't decrease as expected, and the model's accuracy on the validation set doesn't improve. A very high learning rate can cause the model to overshoot the optimal point during training. Inappropriate The loss function may not be well-suited for the problem you're trying to solve. Different optimizers behave differently, and some may not be suited for specific types of tasks.

Solution -

- Adjust Learning Rate: Begin by lowering the learning rate. If it's too high, the model can overshoot the minimum point. Conversely, if it's too low, the model may train extremely slowly or get stuck in a local minimum.

- Change Optimization Algorithms: Algorithms like Adam, RMSProp, or SGD have different behaviors. Experiment with them to see which one works best for your specific dataset and model.

- Verify Loss Function: Ensure that the loss function is appropriate for the type of task you are trying to achieve. For instance, for a binary classification task, use Binary Cross-Entropy, while for multi-class classification, use Categorical Cross-Entropy.

GPU Memory Errors

Training gets interrupted because the GPU runs out of memory. This is a common issue, especially when using large models or when the batch size is too big. A larger batch size requires the GPU to store more data at once. Some deep learning models, especially those with many layers or parameters, can be memory-intensive. Storing too many auxiliary operations or data can take up GPU memory.

Solution -

- Reduce Batch Size: By using a smaller batch size, you'll reduce the amount of data the GPU needs to process at once, freeing up memory. This might slightly affect the model's convergence speed, but it's a necessary trade-off.

- Simplify Model: If possible, reduce the number of layers or parameters in your model. Consider using architectures that are designed to be efficient in terms of memory usage.

- Gradient Accumulation: Instead of reducing the batch size, you can use gradient accumulation. This involves forwarding multiple mini-batches before doing a backpropagation, mimicking a larger batch size without the extra memory requirement.

- Memory-efficient Operations: Libraries such as NVIDIA's Apex offer mixed precision training, which can reduce memory usage by using both 16-bit and 32-bit floating-point types during training, leading to performance improvements.

Deployment Errors

Model Loading Errors

One of the most common challenges during deployment is loading a pre-trained model correctly. The model fails to load or throws an unexpected error during loading.

Solution -

- Double-check if the model's architecture during the inference phase is identical to that during training.
- Ensure that all custom layers or functions used in the model are available and correctly imported during the loading process.
- Check the versions of the libraries. Often, a mismatch between library versions, especially PyTorch, during training and inference can lead to unexpected errors.
- If using GPU for training and CPU for inference, or vice versa, verify to map the model to the correct device before loading.

Performance Issues in Production

Post successful deployment, performance optimization becomes crucial. In real-world scenarios, the efficiency of a model's inference time is as vital as its accuracy. The model's inference time is longer than expected, causing delays and inefficiencies in the application.

Solution -

- Implement model quantization, which reduces the numerical precision of the model's weights, leading to faster computation times and smaller model sizes without significantly sacrificing accuracy.
- Convert the PyTorch model to an ONNX format. ONNX is a more optimized and efficient format for deployment, and many tools support acceleration specifically for ONNX models.
- Consider pruning the model. This involves removing parts of the neural network that don't contribute significantly to the output, thus reducing complexity and enhancing speed.
- Re-evaluate the hardware setup. Using specialized hardware like GPUs or TPUs can exponentially boost the model's inference speed.
- Parallelize the inference if possible. Running multiple inferences simultaneously can better utilize available hardware and reduce overall processing time.
- Look into batching. If multiple inputs need to be processed, batching them together can exploit the parallel processing capabilities of modern hardware.

- Cache frequent outputs. If certain inputs are processed regularly, consider caching their outputs to avoid redundant computation.

Errors in NLP projects can occur at various stages, from preprocessing to deployment. The solutions often require a detailed understanding of the data, model, and tools being used. It's beneficial to create robust validation and testing procedures, use version control for data and code, and be methodical in tracking experiments and changes.

Summary

The first thing that we did in this chapter was delve into the application of PyTorch in Natural Language Processing (NLP), covering a wide variety of tasks and models along the way. We investigated the preprocessing of text data by using torchtext. This involved tokenization and encoding, both of which are essential processes in the preparation of data for modeling. We were able to successfully implement these preprocessing techniques by making use of a dataset that was freely available to the public. This allowed us to properly manage special characters and choose the appropriate tokenization approach.

After that, we moved on to the construction of several different NLP models, beginning with a text classification model. We eventually moved on to architectures with a higher degree of complexity, such as sequence-to-sequence (seq2seq) models for machine translation, transformers, and Named Entity Recognition (NER) models. The chapter focused on layer dimensions, input types, and training procedures as it discussed the practical implementation of these models by using PyTorch. We also investigated ways to enhance already-existing NER models and optimize NLP pipelines by taking into account the specific requirements of each model as well as the computational resources that were readily available.

Last but not least, the chapter shed light on potential errors that can arise throughout different stages of the NLP pipeline, and it provided specific solutions to address those errors. These errors ranged from problems with the data preprocessing, such as improper tokenization and character encoding, to inconsistencies with the model architecture, such as mismatched dimensions. In addition to that, we talked about training errors such as exploding gradients and overfitting, as well as inference errors such as out-of-vocabulary words, optimization challenges, and deployment problems. We have armed ourselves with the knowledge necessary to develop reliable and effective NLP models using PyTorch by first recognizing the potential pitfalls that may arise and then proposing solutions to address those pitfalls.

CHAPTER 6: GRAPH NEURAL NETWORKS (GNNS)

Introduction to Graph Neural Networks

Graph Neural Networks (GNNs) represent an exciting advancement in deep learning where neural architectures are designed to operate directly on graph structured data. While traditional neural networks like RNNs and CNNs process data in regular grids like sequences or images, GNNs can handle more complex relationships modeled as graphs. This makes them uniquely suited for domains where data has an underlying graph representation.

Many real-world datasets and interactions naturally form graph structures. Social networks, molecular interactions, trade routes, and knowledge bases can all be represented as graphs. Nodes denote entities while edges capture relationships. Graphs efficiently encode transitive, higher-order, and non-Euclidean dependencies difficult to represent in grids. Graph neural networks aim to harness these rich relational representations for machine learning.

GNN building blocks operate on local graph neighborhoods using recursive neighborhood aggregation and graph embedding. By message passing between neighbors, nodes progressively integrate relational context from a wider receptive field. Various convolutional-style aggregation functions compute feature updates. After multiple rounds of message passing, nodes obtain latent vector representations that encode structural properties.

GNN architectures like Graph Convolution Networks, GraphSAGE, and Graph Attention Networks have been successfully applied to social network analysis, knowledge graphs, recommender systems, drug discovery, quantum chemistry, and other graph-based domains. Problems like node classification, link prediction, community detection, and graph classification can be addressed.

Comparison with Recurrent Neural Networks

While both operate on structured data, GNNs and RNNs are tailored to fundamentally different types of relationships. RNNs are designed for sequential dependencies where order matters - time series forecasting, language modeling, speech recognition. They recursively pass information along a chain, one step at a time.

In contrast, GNNs handle arbitrary, non-sequential graphs - social networks, molecular interactions, knowledge graphs. They allow modeling complex relationships simultaneously rather than sequentially. This distinction makes RNNs suitable for temporal data like text or audio while GNNs fit relational data like communities and chemical compounds. The recursive nature still allows capturing long-range dependencies in graphs.

Comparison with Convolutional Neural Networks

CNNs and GNNs both capture spatial relationships but differ significantly in how connectivity is defined. CNNs leverage proximity on grid data like images, with local receptive fields and weight sharing. Nearby pixels relate more strongly than distant ones.

GNNs operate on general graphs where connectivity is flexible. Nodes relate based on linkage rather than physical closeness. There are no rigid grids or weights sharing. This allows GNNs to model irregular real-world networks - social, biological, financial systems. CNNs still dominate computer vision tasks involving images, video and other regular grids. So CNNs excel at extracting visual patterns while GNNs analyze complex relationships and connections, complementary strengths on different data structures.

Unique Features of GNNs

GNNs have unique properties that distinguish them from RNNs and CNNs:

- Relationship Learning: GNNs excel at learning intricate relationships and dependencies between entities.
- Invariance to Permutations: Unlike sequential models, GNNs are invariant to the ordering of nodes, meaning that the model's output doesn't change if the nodes' order is altered.
- Handling of Heterogeneous Data: GNNs can efficiently handle graphs with different types of nodes and edges, representing various kinds of relationships.

Their unique architecture allows them to capture complex patterns in relationships between entities, setting them apart from both RNNs and CNNs. They offer a rich set of possibilities for modeling connections in various domains.

My First GNN Model

The formation of a Graph Neural Network (GNN) calls for the completion of a number of tasks, such as the installation of required libraries, the preparation of data, the definition of the GNN model, and the training of the model. In the following sections, we will walk you through these steps, including the installation of PyTorch Geometric, which includes helpful tools for working with GNNs.

Installing PyTorch Geometric

PyTorch Geometric (PyG) is a popular library for working with graph-structured data in PyTorch. You can install it along with its dependencies by running:

```
pip install torch torchvision torch-geometric
```

Importing Necessary Libraries

Start by importing PyTorch and the relevant modules from PyTorch Geometric:

```
import torch
import torch.nn.functional as F
from torch_geometric.nn import GCNConv
from torch_geometric.data import Data
```

Creating Graph

Define a simple graph with PyTorch Geometric Data class. Following is an example of a star-like graph with five nodes:

```
edge_index = torch.tensor([[0, 1, 1, 2, 2, 3], [1, 0, 2, 1, 3, 2]], dtype=torch.long)
x = torch.tensor([[1], [1], [1], [1], [1]], dtype=torch.float)
y = torch.tensor([0, 1, 1, 0, 1], dtype=torch.float)
graph_data = Data(x=x, edge_index=edge_index, y=y)
```

Defining GNN Model

Define a Graph Convolutional Network (GCN) model using PyG's GCNConv layer:

```
class GNN(torch.nn.Module):
    def __init__(self):
        super(GNN, self).__init__()
        self.conv1 = GCNConv(1, 16)
        self.conv2 = GCNConv(16, 2)

    def forward(self, data):
        x, edge_index = data.x, data.edge_index

        x = self.conv1(x, edge_index)
        x = F.relu(x)
        x = F.dropout(x, training=self.training)
        x = self.conv2(x, edge_index)
```

```
        return F.log_softmax(x, dim=1)
```

Training Model

Create an instance of the model, define a loss function and an optimizer, and train the model:

```
model = GNN()
optimizer = torch.optim.Adam(model.parameters(), lr=0.01)
loss_criterion = torch.nn.NLLLoss()

for epoch in range(200):
    model.train()
    optimizer.zero_grad()
    out = model(graph_data)
    loss = loss_criterion(out, graph_data.y.long())
    loss.backward()
    optimizer.step()
```

Evaluating Model

Evaluate the model's performance on the same data (in practice, you would use a separate validation set):

```
model.eval()
out = model(graph_data)
_, pred = out.max(dim=1)
correct = float(pred.eq(graph_data.y.long()).sum().item())
accuracy = correct / graph_data.num_nodes
print('Accuracy: {:.4f}'.format(accuracy))
```

The above code will print the model's accuracy on the training data. In practice, you would further split your data into training, validation, and test sets and follow a more rigorous evaluation procedure.

Adding Convolution Layers to GNN

When it comes to understanding the spatial relationships present in graph-structured data, the convolutional layers of Graph Neural Networks (GNNs) play a pivotal role. We are able to expand the receptive field of the nodes of the GNN by adding more convolutional layers to the network. This gives the nodes the ability to extract more complex and hierarchical characteristics from the graph.

Following is how you can expand on the previously created GNN model by adding additional convolutional layers and employing a more sophisticated architecture:

Importing Necessary Libraries

Validate to import the necessary modules and libraries, as shown in the previous section.

Extending GNN Model

The following code extends the original GNN model by adding more Graph Convolutional Network (GCN) layers:

```
class ExtendedGNN(torch.nn.Module):
    def __init__(self):
        super(ExtendedGNN, self).__init__()
        self.conv1 = GCNConv(1, 16)
        self.conv2 = GCNConv(16, 32)
        self.conv3 = GCNConv(32, 64)
        self.conv4 = GCNConv(64, 128)
        self.fc1 = torch.nn.Linear(128, 64)
        self.fc2 = torch.nn.Linear(64, 2)

    def forward(self, data):
        x, edge_index = data.x, data.edge_index

        x = self.conv1(x, edge_index)
        x = F.relu(x)
        x = self.conv2(x, edge_index)
        x = F.relu(x)
        x = self.conv3(x, edge_index)
```

```
        x = F.relu(x)
        x = self.conv4(x, edge_index)
        x = F.relu(x)

        x = self.fc1(x)
        x = F.relu(x)
        x = F.dropout(x, training=self.training)
        x = self.fc2(x)

        return F.log_softmax(x, dim=1)
```

In the above snippet, we have added three additional convolutional layers, and the number of features increases with each layer. Following the convolutional layers, we've added two fully connected (FC) layers to map the higher-dimensional features to the final output space.

Training Extended Model

You can follow the same training process as described in the previous section to train this extended model. Instantiate the new model, define the loss function and optimizer, and proceed with the training loop:

```
model = ExtendedGNN()
optimizer = torch.optim.Adam(model.parameters(), lr=0.01)
loss_criterion = torch.nn.NLLLoss()

for epoch in range(200):
    model.train()
    optimizer.zero_grad()
    out = model(graph_data)
    loss = loss_criterion(out, graph_data.y.long())
    loss.backward()
    optimizer.step()
```

Evaluating Extended Model

Evaluate the extended model on your validation or test data:

```
model.eval()
out = model(graph_data)
_, pred = out.max(dim=1)
correct = float(pred.eq(graph_data.y.long()).sum().item())
accuracy = correct / graph_data.num_nodes
print('Accuracy: {:.4f}'.format(accuracy))
```

The extended model with additional convolutional layers provides a more complex model architecture that can capture intricate relationships in the graph. By adjusting the number of layers and the number of features in each layer, you can tune the model's capacity to match the complexity of the task.

Adding Attentional Layers

The basic idea of attention in GNNs is to assign different weightage to different nodes when aggregating neighborhood information. The attention score often depends on the features of the nodes and/or the edge attributes. Mathematically, it can be represented as:

$$\text{Attention Score}(a_{ij}) = f(\text{Node Feature}_i, \text{Node Feature}_j, \text{Edge Attribute}_{ij})$$

In this case, f is a function that calculates the attention score based on the node features and edge attributes.

Graph Attention Network (GAT) Layer

PyTorch Geometric (PyG) comes with a ready-to-use Graph Attention Network (GAT) layer. The GAT layer utilizes self-attention mechanisms to weigh the neighbors of a node.

Modifying Existing Model

We will modify the existing model to include GAT layers. The given below is the code to implement the updated model:

```
from torch_geometric.nn import GATConv

class GNNWithAttention(torch.nn.Module):
    def __init__(self):
```

```
        super(GNNWithAttention, self).__init__()
        self.conv1 = GATConv(1, 16, heads=2) # 2 attention heads
        self.conv2 = GATConv(16*2, 32, heads=2) # 2 attention heads
        self.conv3 = GATConv(32*2, 64, heads=2) # 2 attention heads
        self.conv4 = GCNConv(64*2, 128)
        self.fc1 = torch.nn.Linear(128, 64)
        self.fc2 = torch.nn.Linear(64, 2)

    def forward(self, data):
        x, edge_index = data.x, data.edge_index

        x = self.conv1(x, edge_index)
        x = F.elu(x)
        x = self.conv2(x, edge_index)
        x = F.elu(x)
        x = self.conv3(x, edge_index)
        x = F.elu(x)
        x = self.conv4(x, edge_index)
        x = F.elu(x)

        x = self.fc1(x)
        x = F.relu(x)
        x = F.dropout(x, training=self.training)
        x = self.fc2(x)

        return F.log_softmax(x, dim=1)
```

Instead of the standard GCN layers, we now use GAT layers (GATConv) for the first three convolutional layers. These layers employ multi-head attention. In this sample demonstration, we've chosen 2 attention heads. Multi-head attention helps the model to capture different types of relationships simultaneously. And, We've used the Exponential Linear Unit (ELU) activation function, which can help the model learn more complex representations.

Training and Evaluating Model with Attention

Training the model with attention layers follows the same approach as the previous examples. Instantiate the new model, define the loss function and optimizer, and follow the same training loop.

```
model = GNNWithAttention()
optimizer = torch.optim.Adam(model.parameters(), lr=0.01)
loss_criterion = torch.nn.NLLLoss()

# Training loop (same as before)
```

Similarly, evaluation on validation or test data remains consistent with previous examples.

After employing attention mechanisms, the model can decide what parts of the graph to focus on, enhancing its ability to detect essential patterns and dependencies within the data. This approach also allows the model to be more interpretable. You can analyze the attention weights to understand what relationships the model is focusing on, providing insights into why the model is making specific predictions.

Applying Node Regression

In the process known as "node regression," we make a prediction about the continuous value that will be associated with each node in the graph. It is possible to use it for a variety of purposes, including forecasting future values in temporal graphs, predicting the importance score of nodes, and predicting a property that is related to the nodes.

In this technique, you will be extending the model we previously constructed with attention layers to perform node regression.

Modifying Model for Regression

Since we are now dealing with regression instead of classification, we need to modify the output layer of the model to predict continuous values. Let us change the last layer of the model to produce the desired output shape for regression:

```
class GNNWithAttentionRegression(torch.nn.Module):
    def __init__(self):
        super(GNNWithAttentionRegression, self).__init__()
```

```
        self.conv1 = GATConv(1, 16, heads=2)
        self.conv2 = GATConv(16*2, 32, heads=2)
        self.conv3 = GATConv(32*2, 64, heads=2)
        self.conv4 = GCNConv(64*2, 128)
        self.fc1 = torch.nn.Linear(128, 64)
        self.fc2 = torch.nn.Linear(64, 1) # Only one output for regression

    def forward(self, data):
        x, edge_index = data.x, data.edge_index

        # Convolutional Layers
        x = self.conv1(x, edge_index)
        x = F.elu(x)
        x = self.conv2(x, edge_index)
        x = F.elu(x)
        x = self.conv3(x, edge_index)
        x = F.elu(x)
        x = self.conv4(x, edge_index)
        x = F.elu(x)

        # Fully Connected Layers
        x = self.fc1(x)
        x = F.relu(x)
        x = self.fc2(x)

        return x
```

Notice that the output layer now has only one unit, corresponding to the regression output for each node. Also, there's no softmax activation since we're dealing with continuous values.

Loss Function and Metrics for Regression

For regression, we often use the Mean Squared Error (MSE) loss. We can define it using PyTorch as:

```
loss_criterion = torch.nn.MSELoss()
```

Training Loop for Node Regression

Training the regression model follows the same structure as before but with slight modifications to handle continuous labels:

```
model = GNNWithAttentionRegression()
optimizer = torch.optim.Adam(model.parameters(), lr=0.01)

for epoch in range(100):
    model.train()
    optimizer.zero_grad()

    # Forward pass
    out = model(data)

    # Compute loss
    loss = loss_criterion(out[data.train_mask], data.y[data.train_mask])

    # Backward pass
    loss.backward()
    optimizer.step()

    # You can add code here to track training progress
```

In the above snippet, data.y contains the continuous labels for the nodes. Make sure to prepare this attribute in your graph data object.

Evaluation

For evaluating regression models, you may want to use metrics like Mean Absolute Error (MAE) or R2 score. You can utilize libraries like scikit-learn to compute these metrics after predicting on your validation or test sets.

Node regression opens up many possibilities for understanding graph data. Depending on what the continuous value represents, you could be predicting anything from importance scores to physical properties or financial forecasts. By integrating attention mechanisms, the model can also provide insights into which relationships and features are most critical in making these predictions.

Handling Node Classification

The task of assigning labels to the nodes of the graph based on their structural positions and the features they possess is a common one in the field of graph analysis and is referred to as "node classification." On the basis of the earlier illustration with the node regression, we are able to modify the model so that it can deal with the node classification.

Modifying Model for Classification

In the context of classification, we would be predicting discrete labels for nodes. Hence, we need to change the last layer of the model to match the number of classes. If we have, for example, three classes, the last layer would look like this:

```
self.fc2 = torch.nn.Linear(64, 3) # Three outputs for three classes
```

The entire model can be defined as:

```
class GNNWithAttentionClassification(torch.nn.Module):
    def __init__(self):
        super(GNNWithAttentionClassification, self).__init__()
        self.conv1 = GATConv(1, 16, heads=2)
        self.conv2 = GATConv(16*2, 32, heads=2)
        self.conv3 = GATConv(32*2, 64, heads=2)
        self.conv4 = GCNConv(64*2, 128)
        self.fc1 = torch.nn.Linear(128, 64)
        self.fc2 = torch.nn.Linear(64, 3) # Three outputs for three classes

    def forward(self, data):
        x, edge_index = data.x, data.edge_index

        # Convolutional Layers
        x = self.conv1(x, edge_index)
        x = F.elu(x)
        x = self.conv2(x, edge_index)
        x = F.elu(x)
```

```
        x = self.conv3(x, edge_index)
        x = F.elu(x)
        x = self.conv4(x, edge_index)
        x = F.elu(x)

        # Fully Connected Layers
        x = self.fc1(x)
        x = F.relu(x)
        x = self.fc2(x)

        return F.log_softmax(x, dim=1) # Apply log-softmax for classification
```

Loss Function and Metrics for Classification

For classification, you will use the Cross-Entropy loss function:

```
loss_criterion = torch.nn.CrossEntropyLoss()
```

Training Loop for Node Classification

Training the classification model is similar to the regression model, but with changes to handle categorical labels:

```
model = GNNWithAttentionClassification()
optimizer = torch.optim.Adam(model.parameters(), lr=0.01)

for epoch in range(100):
    model.train()
    optimizer.zero_grad()

    # Forward pass
    out = model(data)

    # Compute loss
    loss = loss_criterion(out[data.train_mask], data.y[data.train_mask].long())
```

```
    # Backward pass
    loss.backward()
    optimizer.step()

    # You can add code here to track training progress
```

Evaluation

For evaluation, you can use metrics like accuracy, precision, recall, and F1-score. You'll need to convert the log-softmax outputs to class labels, which can be done using torch.argmax():

```
predicted_classes = torch.argmax(out, dim=1)
```

Node classification can be applied to a myriad of domains, including social network analysis (e.g., identifying influential users), biological networks (e.g., categorizing types of proteins), and citation networks (e.g., classifying papers into subjects). The use of convolution layers and attention mechanisms enables the model to capture local and global structures in the graph, making it a powerful tool for uncovering hidden patterns and relationships.

Applying Graph Embedding

Graph embedding techniques are essential for converting graph structures into continuous vector spaces, which can be fed into various machine learning models. By learning the embeddings, we capture the topology, structure, and features of the nodes in the graph. These techniques can further enhance the previously built model by adding a more nuanced understanding of the relationships within the graph.

Choose Graph Embedding Technique

Several graph embedding techniques can be used, such as Node2Vec, DeepWalk, or LINE. In this technique, you will utilize Node2Vec, an algorithmic framework for learning continuous feature representations for nodes in networks.

Install Required Libraries

You'll need to install the Node2Vec library. If you're using Python, you can do this via pip:

```
pip install node2vec
```

Prepare Graph Data

We need to convert our existing PyTorch Geometric data into a NetworkX graph to work with Node2Vec.

```
import networkx as nx

G = nx.Graph()

# Add edges from PyTorch Geometric Data
edge_index = data.edge_index.numpy()
for i in range(edge_index.shape[1]):
    G.add_edge(edge_index[0, i], edge_index[1, i])
```

Create Node2Vec Model

Now, let us initialize the Node2Vec model with the chosen hyperparameters.

```
from node2vec import Node2Vec

node2vec = Node2Vec(G, dimensions=64, walk_length=30, num_walks=200,
workers=4)

dimensions: Embedding dimension
walk_length: Length of each random walk
num_walks: Number of random walks per node
workers: Number of worker threads to train the model
```

Train Embedding Model

```
model = node2vec.fit(window=10, min_count=1)
window: Maximum distance between the current and predicted node within a walk.
min_count: Ignores all nodes with total frequency lower than this.
```

Get Node Embeddings

You can retrieve the vector for a node using the following command:

```
vector = model.wv['2'] # Get the vector for node '2'
```

Utilize Embeddings in Graph Neural Network

Now, you can use these embeddings as input features for your GNN model. Replace the initial node features data.x with the learned embeddings:

```
embeddings = [model.wv[str(i)] for i in range(len(data.x))]
data.x = torch.tensor(embeddings, dtype=torch.float)
```

Train GNN with New Features

Train your existing GNN model with these new features as you have done before.

Graph embeddings can capture the structural and relational information in the graph, making them powerful for various downstream tasks such as link prediction, community detection, and graph classification. The combination of learned embeddings with GNNs allows for a rich representation of the graph, capturing both local and global structural information.

Common Challenges & Solutions

Creating and working with Graph Neural Networks (GNNs) can be a complex task, and various challenges and errors may arise during different stages of the development process. How about we explore some of the common challenges, along with practical solutions to tackle them.

Graph Data Preparation

Graph data can be particularly tricky to work with because it often comes with its own set of challenges, such as heterogeneity, noise, or incomplete information. Unlike structured data, where preprocessing is often straightforward, the complexity of graph data makes it challenging to prepare for analysis.

Solution - To tackle these challenges, the following steps can be considered:

- Data Validation: The first step is to validate your graph data. Ensure that the connections between nodes make sense in the context of the problem you're trying to solve.

- Handling Missing Values: Graphs can often have missing attributes or incomplete edges. Techniques like imputation can be used to fill in these missing values based on the attributes of neighboring nodes.

```
# Impute missing values based on neighboring node attributes
# This is a simplified example and real-world scenarios may require more complex
imputation methods
for node in graph.nodes():
    if graph.nodes[node]['attribute'] is None:
        graph.nodes[node]['attribute'] = compute_attribute_from_neighbors(graph, node)
```

- Noise Reduction: Noisy data can skew the results. Cleaning methods like outlier detection or smoothing techniques can be used to reduce the noise.

```
# Remove nodes or edges considered as outliers
# This is just a conceptual example
for node in list(graph.nodes()):
    if is_outlier(graph, node):
        graph.remove_node(node)
```

- Data Normalization: Features may need to be normalized so that they are on a similar scale. This is especially important if you are planning to use machine learning algorithms that are sensitive to feature scales.

```
# Normalize node attributes
for node in graph.nodes():
    graph.nodes[node]['normalized_attribute'] = normalize(graph.nodes[node]['attribute'])
```

Graph Embedding Challenges

When working with graph embedding techniques like Node2Vec or DeepWalk, choosing the wrong hyperparameters can lead to poor-quality embeddings. This affects the performance of any downstream tasks like clustering, classification, or link prediction.

Solution - Optimizing hyperparameters is crucial for obtaining high-quality embeddings. The given below is how you can go about it:

- Grid Search: Use grid search to systematically work through multiple combinations of hyperparameters and cross-validate to find the best set.

```
from sklearn.model_selection import GridSearchCV
# Define the hyperparameter grid
param_grid = {'dimensions': [32, 64, 128], 'walk_length': [20, 40, 60]}
grid_search = GridSearchCV(Node2VecModel, param_grid)
grid_search.fit(graph)
```

- Experiment and Observe: Try out various embedding techniques. What works well for one type of graph might not work for another.

- Validation: Use a validation set to evaluate the performance of the embeddings on the task at hand, be it node classification, link prediction, or any other graph-based task.

- Fine-Tuning: Once you've found a promising set of hyperparameters, you might want to fine-tune them to further improve the performance.

Model Architecture Challenges

Designing a Graph Neural Network (GNN) architecture can be a daunting task, especially when dealing with multi-layer models, convolution layers, or attentional layers. Selecting the right components and configurations may require extensive experimentation and domain knowledge.

Solution - Starting Point: Begin with well-established architectures as a base model. Examples include GCN (Graph Convolutional Network) or GAT (Graph Attention Network).

- Iterative Complexity: Start simple and incrementally add layers or features like attention mechanisms. Experiment and measure performance at each step.

- Libraries: Utilize specialized libraries like PyTorch Geometric, which offer pre-built layers and models. This can significantly reduce the development time.

```
import torch_geometric.nn as pyg_nn
class GCNModel(torch.nn.Module):
    def __init__(self):
        super(GCNModel, self).__init__()
        self.conv1 = pyg_nn.GCNConv(input_dim, hidden_dim)
        self.conv2 = pyg_nn.GCNConv(hidden_dim, output_dim)
```

Training Challenges

Training GNNs can be tricky due to issues such as overfitting, vanishing gradients, and exploding gradients.

Solution -

- Overfitting: Use dropout layers to randomly deactivate certain neurons during training. Apply regularization techniques like L1 or L2 regularization. Implement early stopping based on validation performance.
- Vanishing/Exploding Gradients: Apply gradient clipping to limit the values of gradients during backpropagation. Carefully initialize the weights of the neural network. Use batch normalization to stabilize the internal distributions of the layers.

Scalability Challenges

Graph Neural Networks (GNNs) have a tendency to become computationally intensive as the size of the graph grows. This can result in longer training times and may even exceed the memory limitations of the hardware, making it difficult to train models on large graphs.

Solution - To address the scalability challenges, several approaches can be considered:

- Efficient Batching: Instead of processing the entire graph in one go, you can batch smaller sub-graphs and feed them through the network. This will reduce the computational load at any given time.
- Parallelization: Distributing the workload across multiple GPUs or even across a cluster can significantly speed up the training process.
- Reducing Model Complexity: Sometimes, simpler models can achieve similar performance with much less computational cost. You can experiment with reducing the number of layers or nodes to make the model more scalable.
- Graph Simplification: Preprocessing the graph to remove less important nodes or edges can also make the model more scalable.
- Use Approximation Techniques: Methods like graph sampling can approximate the behavior of large graphs, thus reducing the computational burden.

Interpretability Challenges

As GNNs become more complex, they can act like "black boxes," making it hard to understand how decisions or predictions are made.

Solution - To improve interpretability, you can:

- Graph Attention Mechanisms: These mechanisms can help you understand the contribution of different nodes and edges in the decision-making process.
- Feature Importance: Techniques such as LIME (Local Interpretable Model-agnostic Explanations) can be adapted for GNNs to explain predictions.
- Visualization: Graph-based visual tools can also be useful to understand the internal workings of the model.

Node Regression and Classification Challenges

When it comes to specific tasks like node regression or classification, GNNs may sometimes underperform.

Solution - In these scenarios, various strategies can be applied:

- Activation Functions: Different activation functions like ReLU, Sigmoid, or Tanh may have varying effects on the model's performance in regression or classification tasks.
- Loss Functions: Experimenting with different loss functions such as Mean Squared Error for regression or Cross-Entropy for classification could lead to better results.
- Hyperparameter Tuning: Parameters like learning rate, batch size, and number of epochs can also be optimized for the specific task at hand.
- Feature Engineering: Sometimes, incorporating additional features or preprocessing the existing ones can significantly improve performance.

Library Installation Challenges

Installing and working with specialized libraries, like PyTorch Geometric for graph neural networks (GNNs), can sometimes be problematic. You might encounter version conflicts, dependencies issues, or platform-specific challenges.

Solution - To mitigate these challenges, follow these steps:

- Check Dependencies: Before installing, review the list of dependencies required for the library. Do verify they are compatible with your environment.

- Version Compatibility: Verify that the version of PyTorch Geometric is compatible with your PyTorch version. The compatibility information is usually available in the documentation or release notes.

- Test Installation: After installing, run some basic commands or sample code to ensure that the library is correctly installed.

Attentional Layers Challenges

Implementing attention mechanisms in GNNs can become a complex task. The intricacy lies in designing the attention layers, optimizing them, and ensuring they work well with the rest of the architecture.

Solution - To handle these challenges, consider the following:

- Use Pre-built Layers: Libraries like PyTorch Geometric often offer pre-built attention layers that are optimized and easy to integrate.

- Test Functionality: Before integrating the attention layer into your larger model, test it in isolation to ensure it behaves as expected.

- Performance Metrics: Monitor metrics relevant to attention mechanisms to ensure that they are contributing positively to the model's performance.

Real-world Deployment Challenges

Deploying GNNs in real-world applications introduces additional challenges like system integration, performance, and scalability.

Solution - To prepare for real-world deployment:

- Design with Deployment in Mind: From the outset, consider how the GNN will integrate with existing systems. Think about APIs, data pipelines, and other integration points.

- Performance and Scalability: Test the model under conditions that simulate real-world load and data volume to ensure it meets performance and scalability requirements.

- Best Practices: Follow industry best practices for deploying machine learning models, such as versioning, monitoring, and rollback mechanisms.

- Cross-team Collaboration: Work closely with software engineers, data engineers, and other stakeholders to ensure a smooth deployment process.

In the end, despite the fact that working with GNNs can result in a variety of problems and mistakes, there are actionable solutions and recommended procedures available to address these concerns. These include the careful preparation of data, the thoughtful design of a model, the appropriate handling of training complexities, considerations regarding scalability, and planning for deployment in the real world. Utilizing the vast ecosystem of tools, libraries, and community support that is available for GNNs is another step that can help in overcoming these challenges.

Summary

In this chapter, we covered Graph Neural Networks (GNNs), which have become a powerful tool for processing data that is represented as graphs. Graphs are a common representation for data. We started off with an overview of GNNs, which included information on what they are, why they exist, and how they are distinct from more conventional RNNs and CNNs. We talked about the fundamental ideas, such as graph convolutions, attention mechanisms, node regression, node classification, and techniques for graph embedding. Having a solid grasp of these fundamental ideas lays the groundwork for designing and making effective use of GNNs.

This chapter placed a significant emphasis on the more hands-on aspects of putting together GNNs. We went over the basics of developing a basic GNN model, including the addition of convolution layers and attentional layers, the application of node regression and classification, and the investigation of techniques for graph embedding. PyTorch Geometric, which helps simplify the process of defining and training complex graph neural network models, was one of the tools that we worked with along the way. The purpose of these hands-on demonstrations was to provide practical experience in the areas of designing, training, and implementing GNNs for a variety of tasks.

In the final part of this chapter, we focused on the difficulties and mistakes that could occur while working with GNNs. We identified specific challenges and provided actionable solutions across a wide range of domains, including data preparation and the design of model architecture, as well as training, scalability, interpretability, and deployment in the real world. These insights equip practitioners to overcome common obstacles and build GNNs that are robust and efficient, tailored to their specific applications and datasets.

CHAPTER 7: WORKING WITH POPULAR PYTORCH TOOLS

PyTorch Ecosystem: Tools & Libraries

The ecosystem surrounding PyTorch is vast and diverse, comprising a wide variety of tools and libraries that have been developed for the express purpose of easing specific challenges associated with deep learning and artificial intelligence projects. Take a look at some of the most important aspects, including:

Open Neural Network Exchange (ONNX) is an open standard that enables developers to interchange models across a variety of deep learning frameworks. ONNX is a component of ONNX, which stands for Open Neural Network Exchange. The ONNX Runtime is an inference engine that enables the execution of model files saved in the ONNX format on a variety of different hardware platforms. Its goal is to offer a fully optimized execution environment that is both effective and independent of the underlying hardware.

PySyft is an extension of PyTorch that makes it possible to perform multi-party computations (MPC). It is a flexible and powerful library that facilitates encrypted, privacy-preserving machine learning by allowing computation on data that continues to remain encrypted and decentralized. This enables collaborative learning without the sharing of the underlying data, which ensures both privacy and security.

Pyro is a probabilistic programming language that is built on top of the Python programming framework and is known as Pyro. It brings together the most cutting-edge techniques of contemporary deep learning and Bayesian modeling, making it possible to perform a vast array of complex modeling and inferential tasks. Pyro offers support for variational inference in addition to Markov Chain Monte Carlo (MCMC), making it an excellent tool for research in probabilistic modeling.

FastAI is a deep learning library that makes it easier to train neural networks to be fast and accurate while utilizing the latest and greatest in industry standards. Built on top of PyTorch, it offers a data preprocessing interface that is both flexible and user-friendly, and it automates a significant portion of the typical tasks involved in model training. The library places an emphasis on simplicity and makes it possible for developers to create robust models with a relatively small number of lines of code.

AllenNLP is a library for designing and evaluating deep learning models for natural language processing (NLP). It was developed by the Allen Institute for Artificial Intelligence (Allen Institute). It encourages a modular and extendable approach to model design in addition to providing a comprehensive selection of prebuilt modules for a variety of common NLP tasks. Because of this, the development and testing of innovative NLP models can proceed more quickly.

TorchVision, TorchText, and TorchAudio are related libraries that work in conjunction with

PyTorch to address specialized application areas. TorchVision is an organization that specializes in computer vision and offers datasets, models, and tools for the transformation of images. TorchText was developed specifically for text processing, whereas TorchAudio is geared towards audio operations. The use of these libraries makes the development process more efficient in their respective fields.

TorchServe is a highly adaptable and user-friendly tool for serving PyTorch models in a production environment. It is able to run on a variety of infrastructure, ranging from a local machine to large-scale cloud deployments, and includes features such as multi-model hosting, logging, metrics, and the ability to measure performance.

Understanding model decisions is essential to building trust and being accountable for one's actions. A PyTorch library known as Captum offers tools for improving model interpretability. These tools enable practitioners to better comprehend how predictive models generate their results. Not only do these libraries increase the power and flexibility of PyTorch, but they also address specific challenges and requirements in deep learning and AI. These challenges and requirements range from the creation and experimentation of models to their deployment and interpretability.

ONNX Runtime for PyTorch

As brief in the previous section, Open Neural Network Exchange (ONNX) is an open standard format for deep learning models. It enables developers to interchange models between different deep learning frameworks, such as PyTorch, TensorFlow, and Microsoft Cognitive Toolkit (CNTK), without losing any of the functionality or efficiency of the model. ONNX Runtime is an inference engine for running ONNX models across various platforms.

The given below is why ONNX Runtime is beneficial for PyTorch users:

- Cross-Platform Compatibility: With ONNX, a model trained in PyTorch can be exported to the ONNX format and then executed using ONNX Runtime on a different platform or with another deep learning framework.

- Optimized Performance: ONNX Runtime is designed to provide a highly efficient and optimized execution environment. It includes several performance optimizations that can take full advantage of the underlying hardware, potentially accelerating the model's inference speed.

- Support for Various Hardware: ONNX Runtime can run on various hardware platforms, including CPUs, GPUs, and edge devices, offering flexibility in deployment.

- Model Interoperability: ONNX ensures that models are compatible across various deep learning tools, enhancing collaboration and sharing.

- Ease of Use: ONNX Runtime provides APIs in different programming languages, including Python, C++, and C#, making it easy to integrate into various applications.

Sample Program: Using ONNX Runtime

Let us take a previously trained PyTorch model, such as a simple feedforward neural network for classifying the Iris dataset, and demonstrate how to export this model to ONNX and run it using ONNX Runtime.

Import Libraries

First, import the necessary libraries.

```
import torch
import torch.nn as nn
import torch.onnx
import onnxruntime
```

Define PyTorch Model

Assuming you have a trained PyTorch model for classifying the Iris dataset.

```
class IrisModel(nn.Module):
    def __init__(self):
        super(IrisModel, self).__init__()
        self.fc = nn.Sequential(
            nn.Linear(4, 16),
            nn.ReLU(),
            nn.Linear(16, 3),
            nn.Softmax(dim=1)
        )

    def forward(self, x):
        return self.fc(x)
```

```
model = IrisModel()
```

Export to ONNX Format

You can export the PyTorch model to ONNX format using the following code.

```
# Dummy input to trace the model
dummy_input = torch.randn(1, 4)

# Export the model
torch.onnx.export(model, dummy_input, "iris.onnx")
```

Load and Run with ONNX Runtime

You can load the ONNX model and run it with ONNX Runtime as follows:

```
# Load ONNX model
sess = onnxruntime.InferenceSession("iris.onnx")

# Prepare input
input_name = sess.get_inputs()[0].name
input_value = dummy_input.numpy()

# Run the model
result = sess.run(None, {input_name: input_value})

print(result)  # Output the result
```

This code demonstrates the process of taking a PyTorch model, exporting it to the ONNX format, and running it with ONNX Runtime, enabling the model to be run in different environments, potentially with optimized performance, and facilitates collaboration with other deep learning frameworks that support ONNX.

PySyft for PyTorch

PySyft is an open-source framework that is designed to enable encrypted, privacy-preserving machine learning. It is an extension to PyTorch, allowing for Federated Learning, Secure Multi-

Party Computation, and Differential Privacy, among other privacy-preserving techniques. PySyft aims to keep data decentralized and to prevent unnecessary data movement, giving more control and security over personal information.

The given below is why PySyft is essential for PyTorch users:

- Privacy-Preserving Machine Learning: PySyft enables training models on data that remains in control of the data owner, withoutÂ the model owner needing direct access. This is key for complying with privacy regulations like GDPR.

- Federated Learning: PySyft allows models to be trained across multiple decentralized devices (or servers), where training data is kept locally and only model updates are shared, rather than raw data.

- Secure Multi-Party Computation (SMPC): It provides tools to perform computations on encrypted data, making it possible for different parties to collaborate without revealing their private data.

- Enhanced Security: PySyft provides an additional layer of security, reducing the risk of data leaks or unauthorized access to sensitive information.

- Supports Various Privacy Techniques: Along with Federated Learning and SMPC, PySyft supports other privacy-preserving methods like Homomorphic Encryption and Differential Privacy.

Sample Program: Using PySyft

Let us demonstrate how PySyft can be used with PyTorch to create a Federated Learning model using a previous example of classifying the Iris dataset.

Import Libraries

First, import PyTorch and PySyft libraries.

```
import torch
import torch.nn as nn
import torch.optim as optim
import syft as sy
```

Hook PyTorch to PySyft

Hook PyTorch to PySyft to enable Federated Learning.

```
hook = sy.TorchHook(torch)
```

Create Virtual Workers

Create virtual workers that simulate different devices or institutions holding private data.

```
worker1 = sy.VirtualWorker(hook, id="worker1")
worker2 = sy.VirtualWorker(hook, id="worker2")
```

Distribute Data to Workers

Assuming you have Iris dataset tensors data and targets, you can distribute them to the workers:

```
federated_data = sy.FederatedDataLoader(data.federate((worker1, worker2)),
batch_size=32)
```

Define and Train Model Federatedly

You can define a simple model similar to the one used in the ONNX example, and then train it using federated learning:

```
# Define the model
class IrisModel(nn.Module):
    # ...

# Create an instance of the model
model = IrisModel()

# Define loss and optimizer
loss_function = nn.CrossEntropyLoss()
optimizer = optim.SGD(model.parameters(), lr=0.01)

# Federated Training Loop
```

```
for epoch in range(epochs):
    for batch_idx, (data, target) in enumerate(federated_data):
        model.send(data.location)  # Send the model to the worker's location
        optimizer.zero_grad()
        output = model(data)
        loss = loss_function(output, target)
        loss.backward()
        optimizer.step()
        model.get()  # Get the model back

        # Print loss if necessary
```

The above program demonstrates how PySyft, when used with PyTorch, allows for Federated Learning, where the model is trained across different virtual workers. The data remains localized, providing an added layer of privacy and security.

Pyro for PyTorch

Pyro is a flexible and universal probabilistic programming language (PPL) built on PyTorch. It merges deep learning with probabilistic modeling, providing tools to model complex relationships, uncertainties, and stochastic processes. The given below is why Pyro is a vital addition to the PyTorch ecosystem:

- Probabilistic Modeling: Pyro allows the creation of rich probabilistic models, incorporating both deep learning neural networks and Bayesian statistics.
- Variational Inference: Pyro has powerful tools for performing variational inference, an essential technique for approximating complex posterior distributions.
- Composability and Modularity: It supports a modular design that enables researchers and practitioners to build complex models from simpler parts.
- Scalability: Pyro has been designed to work well with large data sets, providing scalability for industry-level applications.
- Integration with PyTorch: Pyro takes advantage of PyTorch's features like auto-differentiation and GPU acceleration.
- Customizable: It's designed for both novice and expert practitioners, allowing for high-

level abstractions and low-level customizations.

- Applications: Pyro can be used in various fields, including finance, biology, physics, and AI, for tasks like forecasting, anomaly detection, data imputation, and more.

Sample Program: Using Pyro

For this particular program, you will revisit the Iris dataset classification task and show how to build a Bayesian Neural Network (BNN) using Pyro. BNNs can capture uncertainty in predictions, something that regular neural networks can't do.

Import Libraries

```
import torch
import pyro
import pyro.distributions as dist
from pyro.infer import SVI, Trace_ELBO
from pyro.optim import Adam
```

Define Bayesian Neural Network

The neural network will have a probabilistic twist. You will define priors on the weights and biases.

```
class BayesianNN(pyro.nn.PyroModule):
    def __init__(self, input_size, hidden_size, output_size):
        super().__init__()
        self.fc1 = pyro.nn.PyroModule[torch.nn.Linear](input_size, hidden_size)
        self.fc1.weight = pyro.nn.PyroSample(dist.Normal(0., 1.).expand([hidden_size,
input_size]).to_event(2))
        self.fc1.bias = pyro.nn.PyroSample(dist.Normal(0.,
10.).expand([hidden_size]).to_event(1))
        self.fc2 = pyro.nn.PyroModule[torch.nn.Linear](hidden_size, output_size)
        self.fc2.weight = pyro.nn.PyroSample(dist.Normal(0., 1.).expand([output_size,
hidden_size]).to_event(2))
        self.fc2.bias = pyro.nn.PyroSample(dist.Normal(0.,
10.).expand([output_size]).to_event(1))
```

```
    def forward(self, x, y=None):
        x = torch.relu(self.fc1(x))
        x = self.fc2(x)
        with pyro.plate("data", x.shape[0]):
            obs = pyro.sample("obs", dist.Categorical(logits=x), obs=y)
        return x
```

Define Model

The model is the Bayesian network itself, and the guide will be an automatic guide provided by Pyro.

```
from pyro.infer.autoguide import AutoDiagonalNormal

model = BayesianNN(input_size=4, hidden_size=5, output_size=3)
guide = AutoDiagonalNormal(model)
```

Training with SVI

Set up the SVI object with an optimizer and loss function, and then run the training loop.

```
adam = Adam({"lr": 0.01})
svi = SVI(model, guide, adam, loss=Trace_ELBO())

# Training loop
for epoch in range(epochs):
    loss = 0
    for data, target in train_loader:  # Assuming the Iris data is in train_loader
        loss += svi.step(data, target)
    loss /= len(train_loader.dataset)
    print(f"Epoch {epoch}: Loss {loss}")
```

Making Predictive Inference

After training, you can use Pyro's Predictive class to make predictions and quantify uncertainty.

```
from pyro.infer import Predictive

predictive = Predictive(model, guide=guide, num_samples=1000)
samples = predictive(torch.tensor(test_data, dtype=torch.float))
# Analyze the samples for prediction and uncertainty
```

The above demonstration showcases how Pyro can create a Bayesian Neural Network with PyTorch, capturing uncertainty in model predictions. This capability is highly beneficial in scenarios where understanding prediction uncertainty is critical. Whether it's financial forecasting, medical diagnosis,

Deep Graph Library (DGL)

Deep Graph Library (DGL) is a Python library designed to simplify graph learning models. It leverages PyTorch (and other deep learning frameworks) to build complex graph neural networks (GNNs) more efficiently. The given below is why DGL is a valuable tool in PyTorch's ecosystem:

- Ease of Use: DGL provides higher-level APIs for defining and manipulating graphs, making it user-friendly for newcomers and researchers.

- Efficient Computation: DGL optimizes graph operations and computations, utilizing the underlying hardware to its fullest potential.

- Wide Range of Pre-built Models: DGL offers various pre-designed graph learning models, such as Graph Convolution Network (GCN), Gated Graph Neural Network (GGNN), and more.

- Flexibility: The library is highly customizable and extensible, allowing developers to design new graph layers and models to meet specific needs.

- Interoperability with PyTorch: DGL works seamlessly with PyTorch, taking advantage of its features like GPU acceleration and auto-differentiation.

- Applications: DGL can be used for a wide array of applications, including social network analysis, recommender systems, natural language processing, bioinformatics, and more.

Sample Program: Using DGL and PyTorch

For the practical part, let us use DGL to build a Graph Convolution Network (GCN) for node classification on the previous GNN model.

Make sure you have DGL installed in your environment.

```
pip install dgl
import dgl
import torch
import torch.nn as nn
import torch.nn.functional as F
```

Define Graph and Features

Based on the previous example, let us define the graph and its node features.

```
G = dgl.graph(([0,1,2,3,4],[1,2,3,4,0]))
G.ndata['features'] = torch.tensor([[0.], [1.], [2.], [3.], [4.]])
```

Create GCN Layer

DGL provides pre-built layers for common graph convolution operations.

```
from dgl.nn import GraphConv

class GCN(nn.Module):
    def __init__(self, in_features, hidden_features, out_features):
        super(GCN, self).__init__()
        self.conv1 = GraphConv(in_features, hidden_features)
        self.conv2 = GraphConv(hidden_features, out_features)

    def forward(self, g, features):
        x = F.relu(self.conv1(g, features))
        x = self.conv2(g, x)
        return x
```

Instantiate Model and Set Hyperparameters

```
model = GCN(in_features=1, hidden_features=5, out_features=2)
```

```
optimizer = torch.optim.Adam(model.parameters(), lr=0.01)
```

Training Loop

Assuming you have labels for the nodes and a training loop, train the model:

```
for epoch in range(epochs):
    logits = model(G, G.ndata['features'])
    loss = F.cross_entropy(logits, labels)
    optimizer.zero_grad()
    loss.backward()
    optimizer.step()
    print(f"Epoch {epoch}: Loss {loss.item()}")
```

You can evaluate the model on validation or test data similarly to any PyTorch model. This demonstration shows how to create a Graph Convolution Network (GCN) for node classification using DGL. The library offers numerous built-in functions, models, and examples that make working with graph data more straightforward and efficient.

Utility of FastAI

fastai is a deep learning library that simplifies the training of neural networks using PyTorch. It provides high-level components that can rapidly create and train custom models, making it accessible for beginners, while also providing the flexibility needed by researchers. Following are the main aspects of fastai's purpose and utility:

- High-Level APIs: fastai's high-level interface makes complex tasks like data augmentation, training loop customization, and model fine-tuning simple and concise.

- Learning Rate Finder: One of the powerful features in fastai is its ability to find an optimal learning rate quickly, saving time during the hyperparameter tuning process.

- Pre-trained Models: fastai offers various pre-trained models (e.g., ResNet, DenseNet), enabling developers to use transfer learning with ease.

- Data Block API: fastai's Data Block API allows users to build custom data pipelines quickly, supporting various data formats and custom preprocessing steps.

- Interoperability with PyTorch: fastai extends PyTorch, meaning that all PyTorch functions, models, and tensors can be used within the fastai ecosystem.

- Extensible Training Loop: Users can modify the training loop by injecting custom code at various stages of the training process without rewriting the entire loop.
- Visualization Tools: fastai provides numerous tools for visualizing data, training progress, and model interpretations.
- Support for Tabular, Text, Image, and Collaborative Filtering: The library has built-in support for various domains, simplifying the process of building models for different tasks.

Sample Program: fastai for Text Classification

How about we use fastai to build a text classification model using the previous language translation example.

Make sure you have fastai installed in your environment.

```
pip install fastai
from fastai.text import *
```

Prepare Data

Assuming you have text data for translation, load it into a DataFrame and split it into training and validation sets.

```
data_lm = TextLMDataBunch.from_df(path="", train_df=train_df, valid_df=valid_df,
text_cols='text', label_cols='label')
```

Create Language Model

You will create a language model that can predict the next word in a sentence.

```
learn_lm = language_model_learner(data_lm, AWD_LSTM, drop_mult=0.3)
```

Finding Optimal Learning Rate

fastai's learning rate finder can help determine a good learning rate to start with.

```
learn_lm.lr_find()
learn_lm.recorder.plot()
```

Training Language Model

Train the model using one cycle policy:

```
learn_lm.fit_one_cycle(1, 1e-2)
```

Create and Train Text Classifier

Once the language model is trained, we can use it to fine-tune a text classifier.

```
data_clas = TextClasDataBunch.from_df(path="", train_df=train_df, valid_df=valid_df,
text_cols='text', label_cols='label', vocab=data_lm.vocab)
learn_clas = text_classifier_learner(data_clas, AWD_LSTM, drop_mult=0.5)
learn_clas.load_encoder('ft_enc')
learn_clas.fit_one_cycle(1, 1e-2)
```

Predict and Evaluate

You can predict new examples and evaluate the model just like you would with any PyTorch model.

```
pred = learn_clas.predict("Sample text")
```

fastai simplifies many of the challenges of deep learning, providing high-level abstractions without sacrificing the ability to delve into details when needed. Its integration with PyTorch allows for easy transitioning between high-level fastai code and low-level PyTorch code, making it suitable for both beginners and experienced practitioners.

Exploring Ignite

Ignite is a library that provides high-level interfaces to help with the training and validation of neural networks in PyTorch. It's designed to minimize boilerplate code and make your experiments more readable and reproducible. Following is a detailed overview:

- Handlers and Events: Ignite introduces the concept of handlers and events that allow users to execute functions at different stages of the training loop, such as at the start/end of an epoch, iteration, etc.

- Metrics Library: A wide variety of metrics like Accuracy, Precision, Recall, etc., are available out of the box, reducing the need to write custom code.
- Built-in Training and Validation Loops: Ignite offers built-in training and validation loops, abstracting away the repetitive and error-prone parts of writing training code.
- Easily Extensible: Ignite is designed to be easy to extend, enabling custom functionalities through user-defined handlers and events.
- Integration with Other Libraries: Ignite can be easily integrated with popular libraries such as TensorBoard, Visdom, etc., for logging and visualization.
- Portability and Reproducibility: With Ignite, it's easier to keep experiments organized, enhancing portability and reproducibility of models.
- Device-Agnostic: Ignite code can be run on both CPUs and GPUs without modification.

Sample Program: Ignite for Text Classification

You will use the text classification example from the previous section and build a model using Ignite.

You'll first need to install Ignite.

```
pip install pytorch-ignite
```

Import Libraries

```
import torch
from torch import nn, optim
from torch.utils.data import DataLoader
from ignite.engine import Events, create_supervised_trainer,
create_supervised_evaluator
from ignite.metrics import Accuracy, Loss
```

Prepare Data

Load your text classification data and wrap it in PyTorch's DataLoader.

```
train_loader = DataLoader(train_dataset, batch_size=32, shuffle=True)
val_loader = DataLoader(val_dataset, batch_size=32)
```

Define Model, Loss, and Optimizer

Use the same architecture as the previous text classification example.

```
model = YourTextClassificationModel()
loss_function = nn.CrossEntropyLoss()
optimizer = optim.Adam(model.parameters(), lr=0.001)
```

Create Trainer and Evaluator

Ignite provides simple functions to create training and evaluation loops.

```
trainer = create_supervised_trainer(model, optimizer, loss_function, device=device)
evaluator = create_supervised_evaluator(model, metrics={'accuracy': Accuracy(), 'loss':
Loss(loss_function)}, device=device)
```

Attach Handlers

You can attach functions to be executed at specific events.

```
@trainer.on(Events.ITERATION_COMPLETED(every=100))
def log_training_loss(trainer):
    print(f"Epoch[{trainer.state.epoch}] Loss: {trainer.state.output:.2f}")

@trainer.on(Events.EPOCH_COMPLETED)
def log_validation_results(trainer):
    evaluator.run(val_loader)
    metrics = evaluator.state.metrics
    print(f"Validation Results - Epoch[{trainer.state.epoch}] Avg accuracy:
{metrics['accuracy']:.2f} Avg loss: {metrics['loss']:.2f}")
```

Run Training

Start the training loop.

```
trainer.run(train_loader, max_epochs=10)
```

Evaluate and Predict

You can use the evaluator to run evaluations, and predictions can be made directly with the PyTorch model.

```
evaluator.run(test_loader)
metrics = evaluator.state.metrics
print(f"Test Results - Avg accuracy: {metrics['accuracy']:.2f} Avg loss:
{metrics['loss']:.2f}")
```

Ignite abstracts away many complexities associated with the traditional training and validation loops in PyTorch. Through its flexible and extensible design, it adapts to various use-cases, allowing developers to focus more on model design and less on boilerplate code.

Common Challenges & Solutions

Let us take a comprehensive look at the common errors and challenges you may encounter while working with different tools and libraries in the PyTorch ecosystem. These include ONNX Runtime, PySyft, Pyro, Deep Graph Library (DGL), fastai, and Ignite. We'll provide practical solutions to each of these areas.

ONNX Runtime

Incompatibility with ONNX Version

One of the primary indicators that you are dealing with an ONNX version incompatibility is when the model fails to load in ONNX Runtime. You might encounter error messages related to version mismatch or inconsistencies between the model and the runtime environment.

Solution - To resolve this issue, you need to ensure that the ONNX version used for exporting your PyTorch model matches the version supported by ONNX Runtime. If there is a mismatch, you can consider the following steps:

- Check ONNX Version: Use the following Python code snippet to check the current ONNX version installed.

```
import onnx
print(onnx.__version__)
```

- Check ONNX Runtime Version: Similar to above, you can use Python to check the ONNX Runtime version.

```
import onnxruntime
print(onnxruntime.__version__)
```

- Update ONNX Library: If needed, update the ONNX library to the version compatible with ONNX Runtime.

```
pip install --upgrade onnx
```

- Re-export the Model: Re-export your PyTorch model to ONNX format using the new version.

- Test Again: Attempt to load the model into ONNX Runtime to verify that the issue has been resolved.

Unsupported Operations

When trying to convert a PyTorch model to ONNX format, the conversion process fails. The error messages usually highlight that certain operations in your PyTorch model are not supported in ONNX.

Solution - If you encounter unsupported operations, the first step is to identify which operations are causing the issue. Once identified, you can take the following steps:

- Modify the Model: Replace unsupported operations in your PyTorch model with alternatives that are supported by ONNX.

- Custom Conversion: In some cases, you might be able to write custom code to handle unsupported operations during the conversion process.

- Test the Model: Before finalizing the conversion, run some tests to ensure that the modified model still performs as expected.

- Re-attempt Conversion: Once the model been modified, try the conversion process again.

PySyft

Incompatibility with PyTorch Version

If PySyft fails to initialize, it often signals an incompatibility issue with the version of PyTorch you have installed. Error messages may indicate that certain modules or functions are missing, or that the versions are mismatched.

Solution - Since PySyft is closely integrated with PyTorch, you need to ensure that compatible versions of both libraries are installed. Following are the steps to resolve this issue:

- Check PyTorch Version: Run the following Python code snippet to check the current version of PyTorch.

```
import torch
print(torch.__version__)
```

- Check PySyft Version: Similarly, you can check the version of PySyft.

```
import syft as sy
print(sy.__version__)
```

- Check Compatibility Table: Usually, the PySyft documentation will have a table or list that specifies which versions of PyTorch are compatible with which versions of PySyft.
- Update Libraries: Based on the compatibility table, update either PyTorch or PySyft or both.

```
pip install --upgrade torch==<compatible_version>
pip install --upgrade syft==<compatible_version>
```

- Re-initialize PySyft: Try initializing PySyft again to ensure that the compatibility issue is resolved.

Federated Learning Connection Issues

Difficulty in establishing connections between different clients participating in federated learning. You may face timeouts, connection refused errors, or other network-related issues.

Solution - Networking issues can be complex, but you can try the following steps to troubleshoot:

- Check Firewall Settings: Sometimes, firewalls can block incoming connections. Do verify that the firewall settings on all client machines are configured to allow traffic on the necessary ports.

- Network Configuration: Ensure that all clients are on the same network or are reachable from each other if they are on different networks.

- Check PySyft and Dependency Versions: It's crucial that all clients are running the same version of PySyft and any other dependencies. Mismatch can lead to connection issues.

```
import syft as sy
print(sy.__version__)
```

- Check Logs: Check logs for any error messages that could provide more details on why the connection might be failing.

- Test Connection: Before running a full-fledged federated learning experiment, test the connection between clients using simple PySyft scripts to ensure that basic networking is functional.

Pyro

Mismatch in Probability Distributions

When you are training a model using Pyro, if the training process fails or produces unexpected results, one possible reason could be a mismatch in the probability distributions used. Errors or warning messages might point towards issues with the distribution parameters or their validity.

Solution - To resolve this issue, you can take the following steps:

- Check Distribution Definitions: Review how each distribution is defined in your Pyro model. Ensure that you are using the correct distribution for each random variable.

- Validate Parameters: Do verify that the parameters for each distribution (like mean, variance, etc.) are within the valid range for that distribution.

- Debugging: Use debugging tools or print statements to output the parameters of the distribution during runtime to check for any anomalies.

- Update Model: If necessary, redefine the distributions used in the model to correct any mismatches.

- Retrain and Test: After making the necessary adjustments, retrain the model and validate its performance.

Poor Convergence in Inference Algorithms

When using Pyro for probabilistic inference, you may find that the inference algorithm is not converging to the expected results. Symptoms can include poor model performance, or diagnostics that indicate poor mixing or low effective sample size.

Solution - If you are encountering poor convergence in inference algorithms, consider the following approaches:

- Experiment with Algorithms: Pyro offers a variety of inference algorithms like Variational Inference, MCMC, and Importance Sampling. Try switching to a different algorithm to see if it improves convergence.

- Tune Hyperparameters: The hyperparameters for the inference algorithm, such as learning rate for Variational Inference or the step size in MCMC, can have a significant impact on convergence. Experiment with different values to find the most effective set.

- Use Diagnostics: Utilize diagnostic tools available in Pyro or PyTorch to understand what might be causing the poor convergence.

- Inspect Model: Sometimes, poor convergence is a symptom of issues in the model itself. Double-check your model for any logical errors or inconsistencies.

Deep Graph Library (DGL)

Incorrect Graph Format

If you encounter an "Incorrect Graph Format" error while using DGL, it usually manifests as errors or exceptions when you try to load or manipulate graphs. The error messages will generally indicate that the input graph format is incompatible with DGL's requirements.

Solution - To resolve this issue, you should make sure that the graph is in a format that DGL supports. Following are steps to consider:

- Identify the Format: Check the format of the graph you are trying to load. DGL primarily supports graphs in formats like adjacency lists, edge lists, or even from libraries like NetworkX.

- Use Conversion Functions: DGL provides functions to convert common graph formats into a DGL-compatible format. For example, you can use dgl.from_networkx() to convert a NetworkX graph into a DGL graph.

```
import dgl
import networkx as nx

nx_graph = nx.karate_club_graph()
dgl_graph = dgl.from_networkx(nx_graph)
```

- Test the Graph: Before moving on to other operations, verify that the graph has been correctly loaded into DGL by running some basic graph operations or visualizations.

GPU Memory Overflow

During the training process of a graph neural network using DGL, you might encounter a GPU out-of-memory error. This generally means that the GPU does not have enough memory to accommodate the data and the model parameters.

Solution - DGL operations can be memory-intensive, especially with large graphs or complex models. To resolve this issue, consider the following steps:

- Check GPU Usage: Use tools like nvidia-smi to monitor GPU memory usage.

```
nvidia-smi
```

- Reduce Batch Size: One of the easiest ways to reduce memory usage is to lower the batch size during training.

- Optimize the Model: Consider using a more memory-efficient architecture for your graph neural network. Some models are specifically designed to be more efficient in terms of memory usage.

- Use Gradient Accumulation: If reducing the batch size compromises the model performance, you can use gradient accumulation as a workaround. This allows you to update the model weights less frequently, reducing GPU memory usage.

- Data Pipeline Optimization: You need to assure that your data loading and preprocessing are optimized to minimize memory usage.

Fastai

Data Augmentation Mistakes

When utilizing data augmentation techniques in Fastai, you might observe poor model performance, manifested by low accuracy or high loss values. Additionally, the augmented images may look unrealistic or inappropriate, which can be evident upon visual inspection.

Solution - If you encounter issues related to data augmentation, consider the following steps to diagnose and fix them:

- Inspect Augmented Images: Use Fastai's built-in methods to view a batch of augmented images and assess whether the transformations look realistic.

```
dls.show_batch(nrows=3, ncols=3)
```

- Verify Transformations: You need to assure that the data augmentation techniques used are appropriate for your dataset and problem domain. For example, flipping an image horizontally may not be suitable for a handwriting recognition task.

- Adjust Parameters: Tweaking the parameters of your augmentation methods can often solve the issue. For example, you might reduce the degree of rotation or the scale of zoom.

- Retrain the Model: After making changes to the data augmentation techniques, retrain your model and evaluate its performance.

Learning Rate Scheduling Issues

Symptoms related to learning rate scheduling include either very slow model training or a model that doesn't converge. You might notice that the loss value is not decreasing, or it may even be increasing, as the epochs progress.

Solution - To tackle learning rate scheduling issues in Fastai, consider the following steps:

- Use Learning Rate Finder: Fastai offers a learning rate finder that can help you identify the optimal learning rate for your model.

```
learn = cnn_learner(dls, resnet34, metrics=accuracy)
learn.lr_find()
```

- Analyze the Plot: The learning rate finder will produce a plot showing how the loss changes with different learning rates. Choose a learning rate where the loss is decreasing the most steeply, but not too high to cause divergence.

- Update Learning Rate: Use the optimal learning rate found in the previous step to update your training configuration.

```
learn.fit_one_cycle(5, lr_max=1e-2)
```

- Monitor Training: Keep an eye on the training and validation loss during the training process to ensure that the model is learning effectively.

Ignite

Event Handling Conflicts

When you are using Ignite for training your machine learning models, you may notice unexpected behavior during the training phase. For example, some handlers might not get executed as intended, or they may execute in an unpredictable order. This can often lead to confusion and may affect the training process adversely.

Solution - To address this issue, you can take the following steps:

- Identify Event Handlers: List all the event handlers you have attached to your Ignite engine. This will give you an overview of what should happen at different stages of the training loop.

```
print(engine._event_handlers)
```

- Inspect Event Attachments: Ensure that each event handler is attached to the intended events. Look out for any handlers that may be attached to multiple events or conflicting events.

- Check for Overwrites: Do verify that you haven't accidentally overwritten any handlers, especially if you have attached lambdas or inline functions as handlers.

- Debug: Use debugging tools or print statements within your handlers to check their execution sequence.

Incompatibility with Custom Training Loop

If you have a custom training loop and you're trying to integrate it with Ignite, you may find that the Ignite trainer fails to work as expected. This is usually because the custom code doesn't align with Ignite's design patterns.

Solution - To address compatibility issues between Ignite and your custom training loop, consider the following steps:

- Understand Ignite's Design: Before integrating, it's important to understand how Ignite's Engine, Events, and Handlers work. This will help you identify where your custom logic should be placed.

- Break Down Custom Logic: Try to break your custom training logic into smaller pieces that can be easily managed as separate handlers.

- Attach Handlers to Events: Once you have broken down your custom logic, attach these smaller handlers to the appropriate events in the Ignite Engine.

```
engine = Engine(train_step)
engine.add_event_handler(Events.STARTED, start_handler)
engine.add_event_handler(Events.EPOCH_COMPLETED, epoch_completed_handler)
```

- Test Compatibility: Run a few training epochs to make sure that your custom logic and Ignite's Engine are working well together.

- Review Warnings and Errors: Pay close attention to any warnings or errors that may appear during the integration process. They can provide clues about any remaining incompatibility issues.

The PyTorch ecosystem is vast and rich, offering many tools to facilitate deep learning and AI projects. While these tools are powerful, they can also present challenges and errors specific to their functionalities. Understanding the common pitfalls and knowing how to troubleshoot them is crucial for effective development.

Summary

In this chapter, we began a comprehensive investigation of the numerous tools and libraries available within the PyTorch ecosystem. These tools and libraries play important roles within deep learning and artificial intelligence projects. ONNX Runtime, PySyft, Pyro, Deep Graph Library (DGL), fastai, and Ignite are some of the tools that fall under this category. We went into detail about the specific function and purpose of each tool, such as ONNX Runtime's capacity to convert PyTorch models for optimized inference, PySyft's support for federated learning, and Pyro's expressive probabilistic programming.

The implementation and utilization of these libraries in the context of previously explored projects was the primary focus of the chapter as it pertained to the practical aspects of each tool. We were able to observe how ONNX Runtime enables cross-platform deployment, how PySyft offers machine learning that is privacy-preserving, and how Pyro provides flexible statistical modeling. We used DGL to manage graph-structured data, fastai to streamline training workflows, and Ignite to efficiently organize training code. In order to better understand the capabilities and applications of each tool, we looked at some real-world examples.

Overall, the chapter focused on the potential pitfalls, difficulties, and workable solutions that are particular to each tool. We took a look at typical pitfalls and offered practical advice on how to troubleshoot a variety of problems, such as compatibility conflicts, operational misunderstandings, and customization challenges. Acquiring an understanding of these challenges and the solutions that correspond to them ensures a smoother development process and enables the correct utilization of these tools in the construction of deep learning and AI solutions that are both effective and efficient.

CHAPTER 8: DISTRIBUTED TRAINING AND SCALABILITY

Overview of Distributed Training

The growth in model size and dataset volume has made distributed training a pivotal necessity in deep learning. As researchers push the boundaries of neural architecture design, models easily reach hundreds of millions of parameters. Massive labeled datasets like ImageNet contain millions of examples. Training such models on single GPUs or devices is infeasible today. This gives rise to the need for distributed training.

By spreading the workload across multiple GPUs on one machine or clustered GPU servers, parallelism can dramatically accelerate training. Mini-batches are divided across GPUs, gradients aggregated, and parameters synchronized efficiently. This allows researchers to keep exploring larger models and data volumes. Frameworks like PyTorch DistributedDataParallel, Horovod, and TensorFlow distribution strategies make distributed training seamless on multi-GPU servers like Amazon EC2. However, naively throwing more hardware at training is not scalable. Communication overheads, resource contention, and consistency issues emerge. There is a growing emphasis on systematic scaling - increasing batch size, model size, and compute in tandem. Large-batch training techniques overcome optimization challenges. Hybrid parallelism leverages model, data, and pipeline parallelism. Quantization and pruning compress models for faster training.

These innovations enable companies to train ever-growing models on ever-expanding data. Products can leverage state-of-the-art deep learning, from personalized recommendations to fraud detection. Startups gain access to cutting-edge AI. The research and industry symbiosis enabled by distributed training gives rise to new deep learning applications. But these advances raise sustainability concerns. Training systems consume massive energy, increased further by distribution. There is an urgent need to develop energy-efficient algorithms and utilize carbon-neutral power like renewables for green AI. Ethics must govern innovation, ensuring fairness and transparency in large-scale distributed systems.

Working with Data Parallelism

Data parallelism is a technique used to distribute the training of deep learning models across multiple GPUs. It helps in reducing the training time by processing different mini-batches of the data simultaneously across the available GPUs. In PyTorch, the DataParallel layer provides an easy way to parallelize computations across GPUs.

Brief Overview

Data parallelism involves splitting the dataset into smaller mini-batches, and each mini-batch is processed simultaneously by a different GPU. The model's parameters are replicated across all GPUs, ensuring that each GPU has an identical copy of the model. Once the forward pass is completed on each GPU, the gradients are computed. These gradients are then sent back to the primary GPU, where they are averaged and used to update the model's parameters. Although the concept is simple, implementing data parallelism manually involves managing GPU communication, synchronizing the parameters, and handling the data distribution. Thankfully, PyTorch abstracts most of these complexities.

Data Parallelism in PyTorch

Let us demonstrate how to implement data parallelism in PyTorch using one of the previously learned examples. You will take the example of a simple feed-forward neural network trained on the MNIST dataset. The code snippets below directs you through the process:

- Import Necessary Libraries: First, import the necessary libraries:

```
import torch
import torch.nn as nn
import torchvision.datasets as datasets
import torchvision.transforms as transforms
```

- Define the Model: Create the feed-forward neural network:

```
class SimpleNN(nn.Module):
    def __init__(self):
        super(SimpleNN, self).__init__()
        self.fc1 = nn.Linear(28*28, 512)
        self.fc2 = nn.Linear(512, 256)
        self.fc3 = nn.Linear(256, 10)

    def forward(self, x):
        x = x.view(x.size(0), -1)
        x = torch.relu(self.fc1(x))
        x = torch.relu(self.fc2(x))
        x = self.fc3(x)
        return x
```

- Prepare the Data: Load the MNIST dataset:

```
train_dataset = datasets.MNIST(root='./data', train=True,
```

```
transform=transforms.ToTensor(), download=True)
train_loader = torch.utils.data.DataLoader(dataset=train_dataset, batch_size=64,
shuffle=True)
```

- Create DataParallel Layer: If multiple GPUs are available, wrap the model using DataParallel:

```
model = SimpleNN()
if torch.cuda.device_count() > 1:
  model = nn.DataParallel(model)
model.to(device)
```

- Training Loop: Train the model as usual. The DataParallel layer will take care of distributing the data and averaging the gradients:

```
criterion = nn.CrossEntropyLoss()
optimizer = torch.optim.Adam(model.parameters())

for epoch in range(5):
  for i, (images, labels) in enumerate(train_loader):
    images, labels = images.to(device), labels.to(device)
    outputs = model(images)
    loss = criterion(outputs, labels)
    optimizer.zero_grad()
    loss.backward()
    optimizer.step()
```

By employing data parallelism, you'll observe that the training time decreases substantially when multiple GPUs are available. This approach allows for leveraging the full power of the available hardware and is an essential technique for training large-scale deep learning models efficiently.

Explore Multi-GPU Training

Multi-GPU training is a common practice to scale deep learning applications by leveraging multiple GPUs on a single machine. It facilitates faster computation by dividing the dataset into mini-batches and distributing them across the GPUs. There are different strategies to implement multi-GPU training, with Data Parallelism being the most commonly used. However, another popular approach is Model Parallelism, where different parts of a model run on different GPUs. You will explore both.

Multi-GPU Training using Data Parallelism

Data Parallelism is a process where a single model is replicated on each GPU, and each replica calculates the gradients using a unique subset of the data. Once the gradients are computed, they are averaged across all GPUs and used to update the model. Following is a step-by-step practical walkthrough to achieve this:

- Verify GPU Availability: Check the number of GPUs available:

```
num_gpus = torch.cuda.device_count()
print("Available GPUs:", num_gpus)
```

- Wrap Model in DataParallel: Use the same model as defined previously and wrap it in DataParallel:

```
model = SimpleNN()
if num_gpus > 1:
    model = nn.DataParallel(model)
```

- Train the Model: The training loop remains the same as in single GPU training.

Multi-GPU Training using Model Parallelism

Model Parallelism splits the model into different parts, with each part running on a different GPU. This strategy is beneficial when the model is too large to fit in a single GPU.

The given below is an example of model parallelism where we divide a larger model across two GPUs:

Define the Model with Parallelism

```
class ParallelNN(nn.Module):
    def __init__(self):
        super(ParallelNN, self).__init__()
        self.part1 = nn.Sequential(
```

```
        nn.Linear(28*28, 1024),
        nn.ReLU()
    ).to('cuda:0')
    self.part2 = nn.Sequential(
        nn.Linear(1024, 512),
        nn.ReLU()
    ).to('cuda:1')
    self.part3 = nn.Linear(512, 10).to('cuda:1')

  def forward(self, x):
    x = x.view(x.size(0), -1)
    x = self.part1(x)
    x = x.to('cuda:1')
    x = self.part2(x)
    x = self.part3(x)
    return x
```

Training Loop

```
model = ParallelNN()
criterion = nn.CrossEntropyLoss()
optimizer = torch.optim.Adam(model.parameters())

for epoch in range(5):
  for images, labels in train_loader:
    images, labels = images.to('cuda:0'), labels.to('cuda:1')
    outputs = model(images)
    loss = criterion(outputs, labels)
    optimizer.zero_grad()
    loss.backward()
    optimizer.step()
```

Key Considerations

- Proper synchronization is required to ensure that the different parts of the model running on various GPUs are in sync.
- Transferring data between GPUs can lead to communication overhead, impacting the speed-up gains.
- The model parallelism strategy is sensitive to the specific hardware and interconnect bandwidth between GPUs.

When your model is small enough to run on a single GPU, data parallelism is easier to implement and performs better than other methods. Model Parallelism, on the other hand, is useful when working with exceptionally large models that cannot be stored in a single GPU at the same time. It is essential to have a solid understanding of these strategies as well as their applications in order to scale deep learning training effectively across multiple GPUs.

Cluster Training Concepts

Cluster training or multi-node training involves distributing the training of a deep learning model across several machines (nodes) equipped with one or more GPUs. This technique is essential when dealing with massive datasets and complex models that would be otherwise impractical to train on a single machine. While multi-GPU training focuses on parallelism within a single machine, multi-node training scales the training process across several machines.

Distributed Training Architecture

Centralized Architecture

In a centralized architecture, there's a parameter server that holds the master copy of the model parameters. The worker nodes compute gradients and send them to the parameter server, which updates the model and sends back the new parameters. This server can be a bottleneck, particularly when the number of nodes increases.

Decentralized Architecture

In decentralized architectures, there's no central server, and nodes communicate directly with each other. This architecture can be more scalable and fault-tolerant.

The choice depends on the scale needs, infrastructure, and level of reliability required. Hybrid approaches are also possible. The architecture affects scalability, fault tolerance, and efficiency of distributed training.

Distributed Data Parallelism

Distributed data parallelism extends the concept of data parallelism to multiple nodes. The model is replicated on each GPU of every machine, and the dataset is split into mini-batches and distributed across the nodes. After computing gradients, they are averaged across all GPUs on all nodes and used to update the model.

Synchronization Methods

Synchronous Training

In synchronous training, all nodes must wait until every node has computed its gradients before proceeding to the next iteration. This ensures consistency but can lead to idle time if one node is slower than the others.

Asynchronous Training

In asynchronous training, nodes do not wait for each other. They compute gradients and update parameters independently. This can lead to faster training but risks inconsistency between nodes.

Communication Strategies

All-Reduce

The all-reduce operation is commonly used in distributed training to sum gradients across all nodes and then broadcast the summed gradients back to all nodes. This ensures that all replicas have the same updated parameters.

Ring All-Reduce

Ring all-reduce is a variant where nodes are arranged in a ring, and data is passed around the ring in a structured manner. This can be more communication-efficient.

Fault Tolerance

In a distributed system, failure in a single node can lead to failure in the entire training process. Implementing checkpointing, where the state of the training is periodically saved, can allow for recovery from such failures. Multi-node training is a powerful technique for scaling deep learning training to large datasets and complex models. It brings together ideas from parallel computing, networking, and system design to enable training at scales that were previously unattainable.

Performing Cluster Training

Cluster training is a sophisticated process and requires careful setup, coordination, and consideration of various technical aspects. We will go through a practical demonstration using

PyTorch and one of our previously covered examples, extending it to multi-node training.

Preparing Code

Setting up Nodes

First, you'll need to set up multiple machines (nodes) that will participate in the training. Ensure that they have identical environments and that PyTorch is installed on each one.

Network Configuration

Ensure that all nodes can communicate with each other over the network. You might need to configure firewalls or other network settings.

Initialize Distributed Environment

Use torch.distributed.launch to launch the training script across nodes. Modify your main script to include:

```
import torch.distributed as dist
from torch.nn.parallel import DistributedDataParallel

def main():
    dist.init_process_group(backend='nccl')
    # Your code here

if __name__ == '__main__':
    main()
```

Use Distributed Data Parallelism

Replace your model instantiation with the DistributedDataParallel (DDP) wrapper:

```
model = MyModel()
model = DistributedDataParallel(model)
```

Prepare DataLoaders

Adjust your DataLoaders to split data across nodes:

```
from torch.utils.data.distributed import DistributedSampler
```

```
sampler = DistributedSampler(dataset)
loader = DataLoader(dataset, sampler=sampler, batch_size=batch_size)
```

Launching Training

Writing Launch Script

Create a shell script to run your training script across nodes. This might look something like:

```
#!/bin/bash
python -m torch.distributed.launch --nproc_per_node=NUM_GPUs_PER_NODE --
use_env train.py
```

Executing on Each Node

You must execute the above script on each node participating in the training. Depending on your cluster setup, you may use tools like mpirun or write custom scripts to launch the process on all nodes.

Monitoring and Debugging

Monitoring

You can monitor the training process using tools like TensorBoard or by logging output to a centralized location.

Debugging

Debugging distributed training can be more challenging. Consider logging key events, using debuggers like pdb, and careful testing of components.

Performance Optimization Techniques

Optimizing training speed is an essential aspect of deep learning, especially in distributed environments where resources need to be efficiently utilized. Given below are some techniques, along with practical examples, to help you achieve this using the PyTorch environment. You will build upon the multi-node cluster training example previously learned.

Efficient Data Loading

Utilize Multiple Workers

Using multi-threading for data loading can dramatically reduce the bottlenecks:

```
from torch.utils.data import DataLoader

loader = DataLoader(dataset, batch_size=batch_size, num_workers=4)
```

Pin Memory
For GPU training, pinning memory can speed up host to device transfer:

```
loader = DataLoader(dataset, batch_size=batch_size, pin_memory=True)
```

Model Parallelism

If the model is too large to fit in a single GPU, you can divide it across multiple GPUs:

```
class ParallelModel(nn.Module):
    def __init__(self, part1, part2):
        self.part1 = part1.to('cuda:0')
        self.part2 = part2.to('cuda:1')

    def forward(self, x):
        x = self.part1(x)
        return self.part2(x)
```

Mixed Precision Training

Mixed precision training uses float16 arithmetic to accelerate training, and it can be implemented using PyTorch's native AMP (Automatic Mixed Precision):

```
from torch.cuda.amp import autocast, GradScaler

scaler = GradScaler()

with autocast():
    output = model(input)
    loss = loss_fn(output, target)
```

```
scaler.scale(loss).backward()
scaler.step(optimizer)
scaler.update()
```

Utilize Efficient Convolutional Algorithms

PyTorch allows the selection of efficient algorithms for convolutions. Setting torch.backends.cudnn.benchmark = True enables this:

```
torch.backends.cudnn.benchmark = True
```

Gradient Accumulation

Rather than updating the weights after each mini-batch, you can accumulate the gradients over multiple mini-batches and then perform the update:

```
accumulation_steps = 4
loss = loss_fn(output, target) / accumulation_steps
loss.backward()

if (batch_idx + 1) % accumulation_steps == 0:
    optimizer.step()
    optimizer.zero_grad()
```

Asynchronous Data Transfer and Processing

Overlap data transfer with computation using non-blocking calls:

```
input = input.to('cuda:0', non_blocking=True)
target = target.to('cuda:0', non_blocking=True)
```

Distributed Optimizers

In a distributed setting, you can use distributed optimizers like torch.nn.parallel.DistributedDataParallel (DDP) with overlap communication with computation:

```
model = DistributedDataParallel(model, bucket_cap_mb=50)
```

Profiling Tools

Utilize PyTorch's native profiler to identify bottlenecks:

```
with torch.profiler.profile(schedule=torch.profiler.schedule(wait=2, warmup=3, active=5), record_shapes=True) as prof:
    train_model()

prof.export_chrome_trace("trace.json")
```

Final Remarks

These optimization techniques can be applied to any previous model we've learned, whether it's a GNN model, text classification, or machine translation. Remember, the effectiveness of each technique can vary based on the specific model, data, and hardware, so experimenting with different combinations and using profiling tools can be essential in finding the optimal configuration.

Common Challenges & Solutions

When working with distributed training and scalability in deep learning and AI projects, various errors and challenges can arise. Below, you will explore some of the common errors and provide practical solutions for each.

CUDA Memory Errors

Error - Running out of GPU memory is a common error, especially when working with large models and data.

Solution -

- Reduce the Batch Size: A smaller batch size requires less GPU memory.
- Use Gradient Accumulation: Allows for smaller batch sizes without losing the benefits of larger batch sizes.
- Utilize Mixed Precision Training: This can save memory by using a mix of float16 and float32.

Data Loading Bottlenecks

Error - If data loading is not optimized, it can become a bottleneck and slow down the entire training process.

Solution -

- Use Multiple Workers: PyTorch's DataLoader allows you to specify the number of worker threads to preload the data.
- Pin Memory: Using pinned memory can speed up data transfer between the CPU and GPU.

Communication Overheads in Multi-GPU Training

Error - In multi-GPU training, communication overhead can slow down the training.

Solution -

- Use Efficient Communication Libraries: Tools like NCCL are optimized for GPU-to-GPU communications.
- Overlap Communication with Computation: Techniques like asynchronous data transfer can help.

Model Not Converging in Distributed Training

Error - Sometimes, models may fail to converge when trained in a distributed environment.

Solution -

- Ensure Synchronization: Utilize synchronized Batch Normalization or properly synchronize gradients.
- Adjust Learning Rate: The learning rate may need to be scaled appropriately for the number of GPUs.

Deadlocks in Multi-GPU Training

Error - Deadlocks can occur in multi-GPU training, causing the training process to hang indefinitely.

Solution -

- Debug with NCCL Environment Variables: Setting NCCL_DEBUG=INFO can help identify the issue.

- Ensure Proper Device Placement: You need to assure that that tensors and models are placed on the correct device.

Errors with Mixed Precision Training

Error - Mixed precision training can sometimes cause numerical instability.

Solution -

- PyTorch's AMP: Automatic Mixed Precision (AMP) helps manage mixed precision training.
- Monitor Loss Scaling: Carefully monitoring and adjusting the loss scaling can prevent numerical issues.

Errors in Cluster Training

Error - Setting up multi-node training can be complex, leading to various errors.

Solution -

- Use Distributed Launch Utility: Tools like torch.distributed.launch can help set up distributed training.
- Ensure Network Connectivity: All nodes must have proper network connectivity, and firewalls should not block communication.

Profiling Overheads

Error - Using profilers can sometimes add overhead, affecting the performance measurement.

Solution -

- Use Lightweight Profilers: PyTorch's built-in profiler is designed to minimize overhead.
- Profile Only Critical Sections: Profile the parts of the code that are essential to minimize the impact on performance.

Model Parallelism Challenges

Error - Implementing model parallelism across devices can be tricky and error-prone.

Solution -

- Use PyTorch's nn.DataParallel or nn.DistributedDataParallel: These wrappers handle many complexities of model parallelism.

Version and Compatibility Issues

Error - Different versions of PyTorch, CUDA, or other libraries might cause compatibility issues.

Solution -

- Ensure Compatibility: Do verify to use compatible versions of all libraries and tools.
- Follow Official Guides: Always refer to the official documentation for installation and configuration.

By understanding these common errors and challenges, and implementing the suggested solutions, you can efficiently tackle issues related to distributed training and scalability.

Summary

In this chapter, we delved into the essential aspects of distributed training and scalability for deep learning and AI projects using PyTorch. We started by understanding the necessity of distributed training and how it helps in handling larger datasets and complex models. Various techniques such as data parallelism were introduced to distribute the computation across different devices, maximizing the utilization of hardware resources. We explored multi-GPU training, which enables training models on multiple GPUs simultaneously, thus accelerating the training process.

Following that, we ventured into the world of cluster training or multi-node training, which extends the model training across multiple machines. This approach allows for even more parallelism, further enhancing the capacity to handle complex and large-scale tasks. We provided practical demonstrations for achieving cluster training using previous examples, and covered techniques to optimize training speed, from efficient data loading to minimizing communication overhead. Different strategies were explained, like using multiple workers in data loading, pinned memory, and asynchronous data transfer.

The chapter concluded by outlining potential errors and challenges that might be encountered in distributed training and scalability. We provided comprehensive solutions to tackle common issues such as CUDA memory errors, data loading bottlenecks, communication overhead in multi-GPU training, model non-convergence, deadlocks, numerical instability in mixed precision training, challenges in cluster training, profiling overheads, model parallelism challenges, and version compatibility issues. Practical insights and tools were offered to effectively overcome these hurdles, leading to a more streamlined and efficient implementation of distributed training using PyTorch.

CHAPTER 9: MOBILE AND EMBEDDED DEPLOYMENT

PyTorch for Mobile and Embedded System

The introduction of PyTorch in the realm of mobile and embedded development marks a significant advancement in the field of deep learning and artificial intelligence. With the continuous growth of mobile devices and embedded systems, there is a rising need to execute complex AI models on resource-constrained platforms. PyTorch's arrival in this area is a response to this need, and it offers a plethora of opportunities and future possibilities.

PyTorch on Mobile Devices

- On-Device Inference: With PyTorch Mobile, developers can run pre-trained deep learning models on mobile devices. This enables the deployment of sophisticated AI models without relying on a continuous internet connection to a server, thus reducing latency and improving privacy.
- Optimization for Mobile Hardware: PyTorch has introduced libraries and tools that are optimized to run on various mobile processors, taking advantage of specific hardware capabilities to enhance performance. This includes utilizing specialized hardware such as Neural Processing Units (NPUs) and Graphics Processing Units (GPUs) found in modern smartphones.
- Cross-Platform Development: PyTorch provides tools to support both Android and iOS platforms, making it easier for developers to build applications that work seamlessly across different mobile ecosystems.

PyTorch in Embedded Systems

- Real-Time Applications: PyTorch's ability to run on embedded systems has opened new possibilities for real-time applications, such as robotics, drones, and IoT devices. By processing data locally, these systems can make immediate decisions without the need to transmit data to a central server.
- Energy Efficiency: PyTorch's optimization for various embedded platforms ensures that the models can run with minimal power consumption. This is vital for battery-powered devices, where energy efficiency is a key consideration.
- Customization and Flexibility: With PyTorch, developers have the flexibility to design and fine-tune models according to the specific requirements and constraints of an embedded platform. This includes selecting appropriate model architectures, quantization, and pruning techniques that align with the device's computational and memory capabilities.

Future Possibilities

- Edge AI: PyTorch's presence in mobile and embedded systems lays the foundation for Edge AI, where data processing and decision-making happen at the device level. This can revolutionize industries such as healthcare, manufacturing, and transportation.

- Personalized Experiences: On-device AI can enable more personalized user experiences by processing data locally, ensuring privacy and customization according to individual preferences.

- Integration with Other Technologies: The synergy between PyTorch and other emerging technologies, such as Augmented Reality (AR) and Virtual Reality (VR), can lead to innovative applications that seamlessly blend the virtual and physical worlds.

In sum, PyTorch's arrival in the mobile and embedded development domain not only addresses current demands but also paves the way for transformative applications and innovations. Its flexibility, optimization, and cross-platform support equip developers with the necessary tools to explore and implement cutting-edge solutions that can redefine the interaction between humans, devices, and the world around us.

Conversion to TorchScript Models

While PyTorch models are defined using Python, for deployment to production environments like mobile, embedded systems, or scalable server architectures, Python dependency can be problematic.

This is where TorchScript comes in. It provides:

- Serializing PyTorch models into an intermediate representation that can be understood, optimized and run in non-Python environments like C++.

- Removes Python dependency, allowing deployment to platforms where Python is unavailable.

- Execution speedups from optimizations like model pruning andcompiler optimizations.

- Integration with platforms like PyTorch Mobile to deploy to iOS and Android apps.

- Ability to save models for inference, eliminating the need to retrain each time.

Let us consider the previously built model and convert it to TorchScript. The process involves the following steps:

Importing Libraries

First, we need to import the necessary libraries.

```
import torch
import torch.nn as nn
```

Defining Model

Next, you will define the original GNN model. The given below is a simplified version:

```
class GNNModel(nn.Module):
    def __init__(self, input_dim, hidden_dim, output_dim):
        super(GNNModel, self).__init__()
        self.conv1 = GraphConv(input_dim, hidden_dim)
        self.conv2 = GraphConv(hidden_dim, output_dim)

    def forward(self, data):
        x, edge_index = data.x, data.edge_index
        x = self.conv1(x, edge_index)
        x = torch.relu(x)
        x = self.conv2(x, edge_index)
        return x
```

Creating Instance of the Model

You will instantiate the GNN model with the desired dimensions.

```
model = GNNModel(input_dim=64, hidden_dim=128, output_dim=2)
```

Converting to TorchScript using Tracing

TorchScript provides two modes for converting a PyTorch model: tracing and scripting. Tracing is the simpler method and works by running the model once and recording the operations performed.

```
# Generate some dummy input data
dummy_data = torch.randn(10, 64) # Assume 10 nodes, each with 64 features

# Use the torch.jit.trace function to convert the model
traced_model = torch.jit.trace(model, dummy_data)

# Save the traced model
traced_model.save("gnn_model.pt")
```

Converting to TorchScript using Scripting

Alternatively, we can use scripting, which analyzes the Python code and compiles it to TorchScript. It's more robust but might require some code modifications.

```
# Convert the model using the torch.jit.script function
scripted_model = torch.jit.script(model)

# Save the scripted model
scripted_model.save("gnn_model_scripted.pt")
```

Loading and Running TorchScript Model

Once the model is converted and saved, we can load and run it independently from the Python environment:

```
# Load the model
loaded_model = torch.jit.load("gnn_model.pt")

# Run the model with some input data
output = loaded_model(dummy_data)
Considerations
```

Not all PyTorch functions and modules are supported in TorchScript and also the debugging TorchScript can be more challenging, hence make sure the original PyTorch model is working correctly before converting.

Deploying Model on Android

Deploying a PyTorch model on Android is a remarkable advancement that allows machine learning applications to be integrated into mobile devices. Here's how to take the TorchScript model created in the previous section and deploy it on an Android device. This process involves several key steps:

Install Android Development Environment

Before deploying the model on an Android device, you need to have Android Studio installed. Android Studio is the official integrated development environment (IDE) for Android development. Follow the instructions on the official website to install Android Studio in order to get started with creating a new android project.

Create Android Project

Once Android Studio is installed, you'll create a new Android project as below:

- Open Android Studio and click on "Start a new Android Studio project."
- Choose an appropriate template, such as "Empty Activity."
- Set the project name, save location, and other details.
- Select the target Android versions. It's generally a good idea to target recent versions of the Android operating system.
- Click "Finish" to create the project.

Include PyTorch Mobile Libraries

PyTorch provides specific libraries for mobile deployment, including Android. You need to include these libraries in your project as below:

- Open the build.gradle file for your app module.
- Add the following dependencies for PyTorch mobile:

```
implementation 'org.pytorch:pytorch_android:1.9.0'
implementation 'org.pytorch:pytorch_android_torchvision:1.9.0'
Sync the project to download and include the libraries.
```

Add TorchScript Model

The TorchScript model file (e.g., "gnn_model.pt") must be added to the Android project. The model file can be included with the project as below:

- Create a folder named assets in the src/main directory of your app module.
- Copy the "gnn_model.pt" file into the assets folder.

Load and Run Model in Android Code

- You can now write Android code to load and run the TorchScript model.
- Open the main activity file (e.g., MainActivity.java).
- Add code to load the model. You can use PyTorch's Android library for this:

```
import org.pytorch.Module;
import org.pytorch.Tensor;
import org.pytorch.torchvision.TensorImageUtils;

...

Module module;

@Override
protected void onCreate(Bundle savedInstanceState) {
  super.onCreate(savedInstanceState);
  setContentView(R.layout.activity_main);

  // Load TorchScript model
  module = Module.load(assetFilePath(this, "gnn_model.pt"));
}

public static String assetFilePath(Context context, String assetName) throws
IOException {
```

```
  File file = new File(context.getFilesDir(), assetName);
  // code to extract the asset to the file...
  return file.getAbsolutePath();
}
```

- To run the model with some input data, you can use code like this:

```
float[] inputData = new float[10 * 64]; // Example input data
Tensor inputTensor = Tensor.fromBlob(inputData, new long[]{10, 64});

// Run the model
Tensor outputTensor = module.forward(IValue.from(inputTensor)).toTensor();
float[] outputData = outputTensor.getDataAsFloatArray();

// Use the output data as needed...
```

Build and Test on Android Device

Click the "Build" menu in Android Studio, then "Build Bundle(s)/APK(s)," and then "Build APK." Once built, you can install the APK on an Android device or emulator for testing.

Exploring PyTorch Lite

PyTorch Lite is a stripped-down version of the original PyTorch framework that was developed with mobile and embedded devices in mind. It has been optimized to deliver high performance while requiring a low memory overhead, which makes it suitable for deployment on platforms with limited resource availability. PyTorch Lite provides the core functionalities of PyTorch, but in a more compact form, to enable the efficient execution of deep learning models on mobile platforms.

Key Features

Optimized for Mobile Devices

PyTorch Lite is designed with mobile-first principles. It focuses on reducing the binary size and boosting the speed of execution, providing faster inferences on mobile devices.

On-Device Capabilities

PyTorch Lite enables on-device inference, meaning models can be executed directly on a device without needing connectivity to a server. This allows real-time processing and ensures privacy as data doesn't leave the device.

Support for Multiple Platforms

It supports a wide variety of platforms, including Android, iOS, and embedded systems, allowing developers to write once and deploy everywhere.

Compatibility with PyTorch Models

PyTorch Lite provides a smooth path for transitioning PyTorch models to mobile-friendly formats. Existing PyTorch models can be easily converted to PyTorch Lite.

Integration with Mobile Development Tools

PyTorch Lite can be seamlessly integrated with popular mobile development tools like Android Studio, making it easier for developers to incorporate machine learning into mobile apps.

Sample Program using PyTorch Lite

The given below is a step-by-step example of how you can use PyTorch Lite to convert a PyTorch model and run it on an Android device. You will use the TorchScript model created in the previous section.

Convert PyTorch Model to PyTorch Lite Format

First, you'll need to convert your TorchScript model to the PyTorch Lite format:

```
import torch
import torchvision.models as models

# Load an example pre-trained model
model = models.resnet18(pretrained=True)

# Convert to TorchScript
script_model = torch.jit.script(model)
script_model.eval()

# Convert to PyTorch Lite format
lite_model = torch.jit._recursive_to_mobile(script_model)
```

```
# Save PyTorch Lite model
lite_model.save("resnet18_lite.ptl")
```

Add PyTorch Lite Model to Android Project

Place the PyTorch Lite model file ("resnet18_lite.ptl") in the assets folder of your Android project, just like with the regular TorchScript model.

Add PyTorch Lite Android Library

In your app module's build.gradle file, add the following dependency:

```
implementation 'org.pytorch:pytorch_android_lite:1.9.0'
```

Load and Run PyTorch Lite Model in Android

In your Android code (e.g., MainActivity.java), load and run the PyTorch Lite model:

```
import org.pytorch.lite.Module;

// ...

Module module;

@Override
protected void onCreate(Bundle savedInstanceState) {
  super.onCreate(savedInstanceState);
  setContentView(R.layout.activity_main);

  // Load PyTorch Lite model
  module = Module.load(assetFilePath(this, "resnet18_lite.ptl"));
}

// ...

// Running the model and using the output is similar to the regular PyTorch Android
code.
```

To summarize, deploying PyTorch models on Android with PyTorch Lite involves:

- Converting the PyTorch model to a mobile-optimized .ptl lite format, usually through torch.jit.script + torch.jit.optimize_for_mobile(). This applies optimizations like quantization while retaining performance.

- Adding the PyTorch Lite Android library to your app dependencies. This contains the core runtime optimized for mobile.

- Loading the .ptl model file into a Lite Module in the Android code. This prepares it for execution.

- Calling the forward() method on the module to perform inference, just like regular PyTorch models. The optimized mobile module seamlessly runs the models.

- Processing the output of the model as needed by your app. The results can be used in the same way as PyTorch model output.

Performing Real-time Inferencing

Real-time inferencing on embedded systems is a critical application in many fields such as robotics, autonomous vehicles, and IoT devices. PyTorch, being a versatile and flexible framework, can be adapted to meet the demands of real-time inferencing on embedded platforms. Let us explore how this can be achieved using a previous example.

Setting up the Environment

- Hardware: Select an appropriate embedded system that supports PyTorch, such as NVIDIA Jetson boards or Raspberry Pi with suitable processing capabilities.

- Software: Install PyTorch and the required dependencies on the embedded platform. Choose the right version of PyTorch compatible with the hardware architecture.

- Model Optimization: Optimize the chosen model for the embedded platform using techniques like quantization and pruning, which can reduce model size and improve execution speed.

Real-time Inferencing

You will continue using the ResNet-18 model that was converted to PyTorch Lite in the previous section. For real-time inferencing, you will capture data from a camera or sensor attached to the embedded system and process it using the model.

Capturing Real-time Data

Depending on the application, you'll need to connect and configure the appropriate sensors or cameras. In this sample demonstration, you will use a camera for image classification:

```
import cv2

# Initialize the camera
camera = cv2.VideoCapture(0)

# Check if the camera is successfully opened
if not camera.isOpened():
    print("Error opening camera!")
    exit()
```

Preprocessing Data

Real-time data often requires preprocessing before it can be fed into the model. For image classification, preprocessing might include resizing, normalization, and tensor conversion:

```
def preprocess(image):
    # Resize to the expected input size
    image = cv2.resize(image, (224, 224))
    # Convert BGR to RGB
    image = cv2.cvtColor(image, cv2.COLOR_BGR2RGB)
    # Normalize
    image = image / 255.0
    # Convert to PyTorch tensor
    tensor = torch.tensor(image).permute(2, 0, 1).float().unsqueeze(0)
    return tensor
```

Loading Model

Load the PyTorch Lite model, as described in the previous example:

```
import torch
```

```
lite_model = torch.jit.load("resnet18_lite.ptl")
lite_model.eval()
```

Running Model

Create a loop that continuously captures frames from the camera, preprocesses them, and runs the model on the preprocessed data:

```
while True:
    # Capture a frame
    ret, frame = camera.read()
    if not ret:
        print("Failed to capture frame!")
        break

    # Preprocess the frame
    input_tensor = preprocess(frame)

    # Run the model
    output = lite_model(input_tensor)

    # Interpret the result (e.g., find the class label)
    predicted_class = output.argmax(dim=1).item()

    # Do something with the result (e.g., display the class label on the image)
    cv2.putText(frame, str(predicted_class), (10, 50), cv2.FONT_HERSHEY_SIMPLEX,
1, (255, 255, 255), 2)
    cv2.imshow('Real-time Inference', frame)

    if cv2.waitKey(1) & 0xFF == ord('q'):
        break

# Release the camera and destroy all OpenCV windows
camera.release()
```

```
cv2.destroyAllWindows()
```

Exploring Model Compression

A machine learning model can have its computational and memory requirements lowered through a process known as model compression. The goal is to reduce the size of the model and speed it up without significantly reducing the level of accuracy it provides. This will allow it to be executed on devices that have limited resources, such as mobile or embedded systems. It is especially helpful when introducing large models into production, which is where efficiency is of the utmost importance.

Model Compression Techniques

As neural network models grow larger and more complex, it becomes crucial to optimize them for inferencing efficiency. Given below are some key techniques:

- Pruning - Structured pruning removes entire neurons or filters based on importance scores like L1 magnitude or Taylor criterion. Unstructured pruning zeroes out individual weights. This sparsifies and shrinks models with limited accuracy impact.

- Quantization - Quantizing weights, activations and gradients to lower bitwidths like INT8 or INT4 representation reduces model size. Linear quantization and differentiable quantization make this possible without retraining. Quantized models allow faster inference on integer-only hardware.

- Knowledge Distillation - A small, fast student model is trained to reproduce the output of a large, accurate teacher model. Distilling the 'knowledge' of complex models into simplified models trades off some accuracy for greater efficiency.

- Weights Sharing - Tying weight values across layers encourages sparsity. Subnetworks can share one weight matrix. Sharing reduces parameters without changing model capacity.

- Low Rank Approximation - Approximating weight matrices by low rank factorizations like SVD reduces the number of parameters. The drop in reconstruction quality is limited.

- Architecture Search - Automated architecture search explores model designs balancing accuracy and efficiency objectives. The search uncovers fast, hardware-aware architectures.

- Hardware-Aware Training - Co-designing model architecture for target hardware like mobile CPUs and training for efficiency metrics like latency and power leads to optimized models.

The goal of these techniques is to create high-performance models suited for real-world applications, not just benchmark leaderboards. Compression unlocks deploying PyTorch advancements.

Model Compression using Pruning and Quantization

You will demonstrate model compression using pruning and quantization on the ResNet-18 model that was used in previous examples.

Import Libraries and Load the Model

```
import torch
import torch.nn as nn
from torchvision.models import resnet18
from torch.quantization import QuantStub, DeQuantStub

# Load the pre-trained ResNet-18 model
model = resnet18(pretrained=True)
model.eval()
```

Apply Pruning

You will prune the convolutional layers of the model by removing connections with the smallest absolute weights.

```
from torch.nn.utils import prune

# Iterate through the named parameters and apply pruning to the weight of Conv2d
layers
for name, module in model.named_modules():
    if isinstance(module, nn.Conv2d):
        prune.l1_unstructured(module, name='weight', amount=0.2)  # 20% pruning

# Make the pruning permanent
for name, module in model.named_modules():
```

```
    if isinstance(module, nn.Conv2d):
        prune.remove(module, 'weight')
```

Apply Quantization

Quantization involves converting the model's weights and activation functions to lower precision. You will use dynamic quantization which only quantizes the weights, keeping the activations in floating-point.

```
# Define the quantization configuration
quantization_config = torch.quantization.get_default_qconfig('fbgemm')

# Apply quantization configuration to the entire model
model.qconfig = quantization_config

# Prepare the model for quantization
torch.quantization.prepare(model, inplace=True)

# Calibrate the model with sample data if necessary (not needed for dynamic
quantization)
# ...

# Convert the prepared model to quantized version
quantized_model = torch.quantization.convert(model, inplace=False)
```

You can then use the compressed model for inference, and compare its performance and accuracy with the original model. Model compression can bring significant benefits in terms of model size reduction and computational efficiency. However, there might be trade-offs in terms of the model's predictive performance..

Common Challenges & Solutions

In the domain of PyTorch in mobile and embedded development, several challenges and errors may arise. The given below is a detailed exploration of the common issues and practical solutions:

Model Conversion to TorchScript

Error - Failure to convert the PyTorch model to TorchScript, leading to incompatibility with mobile or embedded platforms.

Solution - Ensure the model is compatible with TorchScript by avoiding unsupported operations and using torch.jit.trace or torch.jit.script to handle conversion. Carefully following the documentation and guidelines on scripting and tracing can mitigate this issue.

Quantization Errors

Error - Quantization can lead to significant degradation in model performance or even runtime errors if not done properly.

Solution - Perform thorough testing using representative data during the calibration phase and choose the appropriate quantization technique and precision level. Ensuring the model's architecture supports quantization and using PyTorch's built-in quantization support can also aid in successful implementation.

Pruning-related Errors

Error - Improper pruning might lead to degradation in model accuracy or unintended behavior.

Solution - Carefully choose the pruning method and amount, understanding the role of each neuron or connection being pruned. Validate the pruned model against a representative dataset to ensure that performance metrics are still met.

Deployment on Android Devices

Error - Challenges or failures in deploying the PyTorch model on Android devices.

Solution - Ensure compatibility with Android by using the PyTorch Android API, following the documentation for building and integrating the model. Debug any device-specific errors by using Android development tools.

Real-Time Inferencing Challenges

Error - Delays or failures in real-time inferencing on embedded systems.

Solution - Optimize the model and the preprocessing/postprocessing steps to meet real-time constraints. Utilize hardware acceleration if available and consider model compression techniques to reduce computational needs.

Model Compression Errors

Error - Loss of model quality or failure in applying compression techniques.

Solution - Carefully choose and apply compression techniques like quantization, pruning, etc., that suit the specific model and requirements. Extensive validation and tuning might be necessary to find the optimal trade-off between size, speed, and accuracy.

Multi-GPU and Cluster Training Errors

Error - Failures or inconsistencies during multi-GPU or cluster training.

Solution - Ensure proper data parallelism and synchronization across devices or nodes. Utilize PyTorch's built-in support for distributed training, and be aware of potential network or hardware bottlenecks that might hinder performance.

PyTorch Lite Implementation Errors

Error - Issues with implementing or running models using PyTorch Lite.

Solution - Follow the specific guidelines and documentation related to PyTorch Lite, ensuring compatibility with the target platform. Debug and test using the appropriate development and runtime environments for the mobile or embedded system.

General Compatibility and Performance Issues

Error - General compatibility issues with the target platform or unexpected performance bottlenecks.

Solution - Thoroughly test the model and the entire pipeline on the target platform, identifying potential bottlenecks or compatibility issues. Tailor the model and implementation to suit the specific constraints and requirements of the platform, utilizing platform-specific tools and libraries if needed.

From model conversion to optimization and deployment, each step may present unique challenges. Understanding these potential pitfalls and following best practices, you can navigate these challenges effectively.

Summary

In Chapter 9, the focus was on PyTorch's expansion into the realm of mobile and embedded development. The arrival of PyTorch in this area opened new horizons, enabling deep learning models to be deployed on a diverse range of devices. This involved exploring TorchScript, a way to serialize PyTorch models, allowing them to run on non-Python environments. Quantization, pruning, and other model compression techniques were introduced, aiming to optimize the models for limited resources. The challenges faced during the deployment of these models on

Android devices and the practical utilization of PyTorch Lite were examined.

Practical demonstrations were provided to show how to convert previously built models into TorchScript, deploy them on Android devices, and work with PyTorch Lite. These processes made it feasible to run PyTorch models on mobile platforms. Furthermore, the concept of real-time inferencing was explained, where techniques were explored to run deep learning models on embedded systems to infer data in real time. Model compression, including quantization and pruning, was practiced, enabling models to maintain accuracy while being small and fast enough to run on resource-constrained devices.

Errors and challenges associated with the above concepts were also detailed. This included potential pitfalls in converting models to TorchScript, deploying on Android devices, implementing real-time inferencing, and applying model compression techniques. Practical solutions were offered to tackle these challenges, such as following specific guidelines, thorough testing, proper selection of quantization techniques, and careful application of pruning and other compression methods. The chapter also emphasized understanding the specific constraints and requirements of the platform for effective deployment. Overall, this chapter provided a comprehensive insight into the essential techniques and best practices for leveraging PyTorch in mobile and embedded systems.

Thank You

Index

Q

R

S

T

U

Epilogue

The journey through "PyTorch Cookbook" has been a multifaceted exploration into the dynamic world of PyTorch and deep learning. From the first tentative steps into tensors and computational graphs to the nuanced mastery of various neural network architectures and the pioneering exploration of mobile and embedded development, the reader has navigated the complex yet exhilarating terrain of contemporary AI technology.

As we reach the epilogue, it's a time to reflect on the learnings and the transformations that have occurred. The book was never about a mere transfer of knowledge; it was a guide, fostering growth and independence, ensuring that the reader can confidently walk on their path, make informed decisions, innovate, and contribute to a rapidly advancing field. It aimed to cultivate a skilled PyTorch Developer and a discerning Deep Learning Engineer, capable of troubleshooting and navigating different stages of end-to-end deep learning development. The chapters were crafted with practicality in mind, blending theory with hands-on examples, demonstrations, and real-world applications. This was not a solitary journey; the reader was introduced to the broader PyTorch ecosystem, learning to integrate tools and libraries such as ONNX Runtime, PySyft, Pyro, Deep Graph Library (DGL), Fastai, and Ignite. This integration of tools equips readers with a well-rounded understanding, not just of PyTorch but of the synergies and opportunities that exist within the AI community.

"PyTorch Cookbook" also acknowledged and prepared readers for the challenges they might face, offering practical solutions and insights into error handling. This readiness to tackle obstacles is emblematic of the book's approach: an honest, transparent guide that doesn't shy away from complexity but breaks it down, making it accessible and manageable. Perhaps one of the most exciting aspects of this book has been its focus on the future. The chapters on mobile and embedded development, real-time inferencing, and model compression open up vistas of possibilities, allowing readers to envision and partake in the future of on-device AI. These insights are not merely informative; they are an invitation to innovate, to be at the forefront of a field that continues to redefine itself.

The completion of this book is not an end but a beginning. The knowledge, skills, and perspectives gained are tools, instruments for the reader to wield as they continue their journey. Whether in academia, industry, or personal projects, the learnings from "PyTorch Cookbook" will continue to resonate, guiding and inspiring further exploration. In closing, "PyTorch Cookbook" stands as a testament to the ever-evolving nature of technology and human curiosity. It's a snapshot of a field in motion, a moment in time captured, but also a glimpse into the future. As technology advances, as PyTorch continues to grow and redefine itself, the principles and practices learned within these pages will remain relevant, a foundation upon which readers can build their legacy.

So, as we close this book, let's recognize that the journey is far from over. The world of PyTorch and deep learning is vast, filled with untapped potential and unexplored territories. It beckons, and it awaits. With "PyTorch Cookbook" as a companion, readers are well-prepared to take the next step, to forge their path, and to contribute to a field that continues to inspire and transform the world. Thank you for being part of this journey.

www.ingramcontent.com/pod-product-compliance
Lightning Source LLC
Chambersburg PA
CBHW081556180726
48282CB00060B/1076
9788119177967